Herbal Pathfinders

Herbal Pathfinders

Voices of the Herb Renaissance

Robert Conrow and Arlene Hecksel

Illustrated by Donna Wright

Woodbridge Press / *Santa Barbara, California*

Published and distributed by
Woodbridge Press Publishing Company
Post Office Box 6189
Santa Barbara, California 93160

Published simultaneously in the United States and Canada

Printed in the United States of America

Library of Congress Cataloging in Publication Data

Main entry under title:
Herbal pathfinders.

  Bibliography: p.
  1. Herbs—Therapeutic use. 2. Herb gardening.
I. Conrow, Robert. II. Hecksel, Arlene.
RM666.H33H47   1983   615'.321   83-12350
ISBN 0-88007-142-7
ISBN 0-88007-128-1 (pbk.)

Photo Credits:

Steven Foster 24, 32, 40, 76
   130, 160, 168, 178, 206, 214
Skywalker 52
Loretta Werner 66, 72
David E. MacKenzie 84
Nick Kelsh 94
Allen Tullos 102
Beth Koch 114

Tom Houston 122
David Harp 138
Greg Barrett 148
Snappy 220
Andrew Teglassy 232
Novato Advance 240
Arlene M. Hecksel 252

Dedication

To the herbalists, in appreciation for their willingness to share with us their joy of discovery, their knowledge, and their friendship.

In this book you will "hear" the authentic voices of the Herbal Pathfinders. Theirs are not formal, studied statements but rather are spontaneous, personal expressions—as in conversation with the reader.

Enjoy "listening" to these voices of authority, spirituality, and experience from the world of nature . . . voices of the Herb Renaissance.

Contents

Acknowledgments

IN FOLLOWING THE PATH of the herbalists we have met many people who gave generously of their time and expertise. Of those who came first, Dr. Paul Lee deserves speical mention and our warmest thanks for instilling in us his great enthusiasm for the herb renaissance. Through Paul, we were soon introduced to Steven Foster who showed up in Santa Cruz one day fresh from the Shaker Community in Sabbathday Lake, Maine. Steven ably examined and commented upon this project from start to finish. His photographs of the herbalists included in this volume provide vivid testimony to his keen eye and sensitive spirit.

Others along the way who helped immeasurably by providing us with contacts and advice include Rob Menzies, Rosemary Gladstar, and Nan Koehler. They are, however, but a few of the many, many persons who shared their time and information. Considerable assistance was provided by Rob McCaleb, research director for Celestial Seasonings, who both confirmed and critiqued certain technical aspects. Also, Dori Smith of *Whole Life Times* graciously contributed a listing of herbal education centers which served as a starting point for our own list.

Without exception, every herbalist we have met provided us with an essential link in our research; without their cooperation, the present volume would not have been possible. Upon two occasions, individuals (other than the editors) conducted interviews. Our thanks to Allen Tullos for interviewing A. L. (Tommie) Bass and Steven Foster for interviewing Norma Myers.

Finally, but by no means least, we would like to thank Howard Weeks of Woodbridge Press. His words of encouragement, his dedication, and his thoughtful suggestions provided valuable perspectives throughout all phases of production.

9

The Herbalists: A Family Portrait

Passed down through the centuries by Emperors and Brahmins, shared at tribal councils, and whispered among the ladies at quilting bees—the knowledge of plant remedies has long been a secret. More recently, scientific studies, combined with an ever-increasing demand for alternative healing methods, have given herbalists renewed courage to speak their minds and their beliefs.

Herbal Pathways is not so much a source book on herbalism as it is a source book on herbalists, the individuals whose knowledge forms the core and substance of today's herb renaissance. Largely, their voices are the voices of individuals who are self-taught and inspired. By necessity, they have dug deep for their knowledge, learning from Indian healers, ancient *materia medica*, or perhaps a grandmother or an uncle . . . somebody who had not forgotten.

By no means are the herbalists we have found representative of all those practicing herbology. Many prefer to

11

keep their work hidden from public view. This is particularly true of those working within ethnic communities or isolated geographic areas. Invariably, the herbalists we have met have been helpful and courteous, opening their homes and hearts in ways unasked for and unexpected. The path they have led us down has been as rewarding as it's been enjoyable, for along the way we've met a "family" of every hue and persuasion. The story of their family tree is the story of herbalism today.

Nan Koehler, who runs a childbirthing clinic with her husband, Donald A. Solomon, an obstetrician, recalls the time in 1974 when *Rosemary Gladstar* first brought some of the herbalists together. "I remember sitting in the upper barn," Nan says, "where we have our clinic offices now, with *Rob* [*Menzies*], *Jeanne Rose*, *Rosemary* [*Gladstar*], and other people from Berkeley—all talking about what we were doing and what everybody was doing and how . . . someday we were going to validate our concerns."

At first, Rosemary's retreats were held four times a year at Rainbow's End Farm, which is located just a little to the west of Sebastopol, California. Then it was called Laney's Ranch, after a woman who wanted to turn the place into an "Esalen North." "I remember how really wonderful it was to be around people who didn't think I was nuts," recalls Nan. "You could say, 'Oh, I like plants, too,' and they would say, 'Wonderful.' You weren't an oddball or something."

For *Nan Koehler*, the "grandparents" of the group were *Rob Menzies* and *Jeanne Rose*. After all, they had entered into the picture even before Rosemary began her retreats. But, of course, there were many others long before *Jeanne Rose* and *Rob Menzies* who had already marked the way. The only difficulty in those days was that it was a hard path to find and an even harder one to follow. But for those who persisted, there were plenty of old-timers around who were more than willing to share their knowledge: folks such as *Stan Malstrom* and *John Christopher* in Utah. And then there were lots of lesser-known enthusiasts in America's backcountry, like *Tommie Bass*, in Alabama, and *Billy Joe Tatum* and *Ellwood Carr*, along with their neighbors in Arkansas and Kentucky.

There were also the Indians who knew the native plants as intimately as anyone. *Rolling Thunder* came to some of Rosemary's retreats and suggested ways to pay respect to the grandfather plant before you started picking. If you fail to ask the grandfather plant's permission to harvest one of his children, you run the risk of violating the basic rights of Mother Earth. Young people such as *Kathi Keville* and her friends listened closely to Rolling Thunder before starting Oak Valley Herb Farm up in the Sierra Nevada, a place where people could grow their own herbs in a respectful manner and experiment with new blends of teas, lotions, and herbal salves.

Throughout the 1970s, a trail of youthful herbalists and experienced teachers found their way to Oak Valley. Usually the visitors stayed for just a few days, but sometimes the days grew into months and even longer. Among those who stayed longer was *Reid Worthington*. Later on, his knowledge would prove instrumental in devising original tea blends for some of the country's largest herb companies.

Despite the camaraderie which flourished at the retreats and on the various herb homesteads, many of the early folks felt a great sense of isolation. *Jeanne Rose* recalls that just a little more than ten years ago she felt like some sort of medieval witch while mixing herbs in her attic apartment near San Francisco's Haight-Ashbury. And the late *John Christopher*, whose evangelistic style awakened literally thousands to the world of herbs, remembered how he fought for most of the last 35 years like a "lone wolf." But now, he commented in a kind of last testament, "The great 'universal mind' has picked it up, and people in various places have started the herb program rolling again. . . . Today the pendulum is swinging our way."

Another forerunner and, perhaps in his own way, the strongest influence of all was Jethro Kloss. In 1939, Kloss published *Back to Eden*, the book which many considered to be the veritable bible of the herb movement. Interfused with the book's deeply reflective spiritual tone was a rare encyclopedia of time-tested herbal remedies. Not until *John Lust* brought out his authoritative *Herb Book* in 1974 was there a book published in twentieth-century America that could compare with the plenitude of *Back to Eden*.

Because such reliable sources were few and far between, support remained limited for those wanting to increase their professional and scientific understanding. In an attempt to rectify this situation, *Dr. Paul Lee*, who had taught philosophy and theology at Harvard and MIT, began the Herb Trade Symposiums in 1978 in Santa Cruz. These gatherings marked the first time ever that herbalists, members of the Food and Drug Administration (FDA), and representatives of the scientific and medical professions sat down to talk with one another. That was also the first time that many of the grassroots herbalists (to say nothing of the professionals) had ever heard of the *physicalist-vitalist* debate that began when Wolfgang Wöhler artificially synthesized urea in 1828.

According to Lee, when Wöhler made urea without a kidney, he inadvertently set the ball rolling that would literally push aside centuries of valuable medical lore and herbal knowledge. Lee speaks of the "vital roots" of herbalism dating back to ancient tribal cultures, to the Greeks, to the venerable Vedic scriptures, and to Chinese medicine. "But," Lee emphasizes, "from then [1828] on, no vitalist could argue for a 'life force' distinguishing organic entities from inorganic ones."

If no vitalist had, to this point, argued so effectively, Lee now set the stage for just such an opening. By inviting some of the top scientists in the country, including *Dr. James Duke* of the cancer research program of the U.S. Department of Agriculture, Lee was providing the necessary scientific and intellectual framework for bridging the gap between ancient classical traditions and the modern world, and similarly, of course, between the *vitalist* herbalists and the *physicalist* FDA. What Lee was actually calling for was not so much a return to the bygone era of Wolfgang Wöhler as the formulation of a more vigorous form of herbology—one that sought less to abandon rational modes than to find their more reasonable limits. The new herbology had to be open to diverse ideas, selecting the best from all worlds in the hope of promoting a refined and up-to-date practice and philosophy.

When the herbalists began meeting with members of the scientific and medical professions, a new synthesis arose, a unification of not only past with present but nation with nation and culture with culture. Healers such as *Dr. Vasant Lad* and *Nam Singh* told of the changes taking place in India and China. They described hospitals where the patient could help decide the type of medication best suited to his or her temperament and need, and medical systems where doctors learned traditional medicine side by side with the more advanced techniques of Western science.

In the New World, we have sometimes been slow to comprehend the values of healing systems different from our own, including those which existed prior to the white man's arrival. The voices of *Sun Bear* and *Wabun, Keetoowah,* and *Rolling Thunder* provide solemn testimony to the American Indians' patient willingness to share their understanding with those who will listen. *Sun Bear* speaks of a unification between native and non-native people that came to him in a vision years back, a vision that told how people would come together to live in love and harmony and to learn self-sufficiency on Mother Earth. They would learn to build their own housing and how to rediscover the timeless knowledge of edible wild plants and herbs.

Today, this vision is echoed in the words of Dr. Halfdan Mahler, director of the World Health Organization (WHO). In calling for health care for everyone in the world by the year 2000, Mahler has announced the organization's decision to include traditional healers, village midwives, and herbalists in its worldwide health programs.

For the herbalists, such proclamations do, indeed, validate the early dreams of *Nan Koehler* and her friends at Rainbow's End Farm. In the ensuing years, while often retaining informal contact with one another, each herbalist has walked a separate path. Each has had to make his or her own way, which if followed by another, might not bring the same results or satisfactions. Yet, as pioneers, they have provided signposts, stepping-stones, and more than an occasional warning for today's generation of aspiring herbalists.

Maybe half of all those interviewed for this book have learned about herbs the hard way; that is, after incurring a serious illness or physical disability, they have set about to find the curative herbs. *John Christopher, Jeanne Rose,* and *Carolyn Hutchinson* are but a few of these. Others, such as *Paul Lee, Ed Smith,* and *Steven Foster,* have learned from a combination of meeting with elder healers and "burning the midnight oil." *Ed Smith* remarks that equally important as his work with the *curanderos* of the Amazon was his reading of "just about every herb book I could get my hands on." Sometimes the herb facts come slowly. *Dr. Jeffry Anderson* recalls that no clues were provided whatsoever about the beneficial properties of herbs during his extensive medical training. Only later, when his patients introduced him to their home remedies, did he start to develop such an awareness.

Certainly, beyond all books, techniques, and personal backgrounds, the greatest of teachers have been the plants themselves. *Louis Saso,* who tends an organic herb garden, remarks that his success with plants is because he sees the power in plants. "I know it can help me," explains Saso, "that's why I can do what I do." And similarly, *Jeannine Parvati Baker* explains, "Most of my relationship with plants has been directly through the plants themselves. . . . But it took me a long time to be able to weed and prune, to discover what was really valuable."

Invariably, the herbalists' contact with plants has led to a deeper understanding and appreciation of the universal mysteries. *Norma Myers* explains that she was not a religious person when she first started working with plants. But because of their influence on her, she was able to see a larger design where humans, animals, and plants were all brought together in one family. "[I believe] that when all these ecological factors were created on this earth," explains Norma, "God had certain laws . . . [and] if people could only live by these divine laws, they could live in health and happiness."

Ultimately the herbalists, like the very herbs themselves, possess individual properties that are best perceived within a larger framework. Each herbalist comes with his or her own story, suggestions, and personal advice. Just as there is no one herbalist who is completely like any other, there is no one remedy or herbal treatment that applies to all. But when heard in unison, the herbalists' voices can be recognized as the anthem of today's herb renaissance.

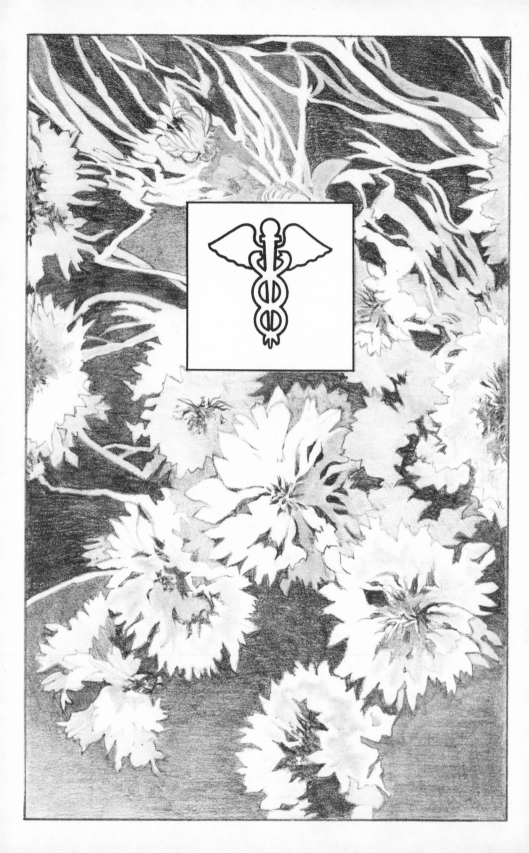

CHAPTER ONE

Roots

THE USE OF PLANTS for medicine is as old as history. With man's search for food came his discovery of the first medicines, and more often than not, they turned out to be one and the same. Although some of the early *materia medica* were divided into the subcategories of *alimentaria* (having to do with food) and *medica* (dealing more strictly with medicines), such distinctions often overlapped. Most herbs qualified as both.

Depending on the time, place, and culture where they are found, herbs can be defined in many different ways. Present-day dictionary definitions usually state that an herb is simply a plant without a "permanent wood stem." For an herb to be so classified it should not produce either a trunk (like a tree) or a thick, woody stalk (like a shrub). Botanists, however, prefer a somewhat stricter definition. They generally like their herbs to sprout in the spring and fade in the fall. In other words, to qualify as an herb, a plant should be a perennial, dying to the ground after the growing season and sprouting again the following spring.

The only problem with all these definitions is that some

19

herbs just don't function that way. Take, for example, typical herbal ingredients such as seeds, mosses, roots, and bark. By more common, if less precise usage, *herb* has come to mean *any* plant that is useful to man. This is no doubt less intellectually satisfying than some might hope for, but it is, nonetheless, an accurate definition within the scope of herbalism as it is commonly practiced.

By whatever name they are called, plants and plant products have provided the mainstay of humankind's medications throughout history. Even as medical practices have changed, the main source of our medicines has remained constant.

Ephedra, for example, has been an effective Chinese folk remedy for about 5,000 years, but only in relatively recent years has its active ingredient been synthesized into the popular decongestant, ephedrine. Similarly, rauwolfia was only rediscovered in this country about 25 years ago, when modern drug companies transformed it into the tranquilizer, reserpine. Its benefits, however, were accurately recorded in the Indian Vedas thousands of years ago.

According to one account, rauwolfia made its return to present-day practice after a Nigerian prince, who was attending a British university, suffered a nervous breakdown. After repeated efforts by leading medical doctors in London to cure the young man, the prince's Nigerian friends sent to their homeland for a tribal medicine healer. After he arrived with a clump of rauwolfia root, the prince made a remarkable recovery, stunning the British doctors. Shortly after this incident, the British physicians began an investigation of the mysterious root that today forms the basis of more than a dozen sedatives and tranquilizers.

In Chapter One, *Paul Lee, Steven Foster,* and *Ed Smith* reveal the hidden histories of plants and point the way to future applications along the herbal pathway. In Lee's tracing of our mythic and historical roots, in Foster's look at our Shaker forebears, and in Smith's probing of the impact of the pharmaceutical industry on Nature's remedies, one is struck by the steadfast perseverance of our herbal ancestors.

Paul Lee traces his fascination with the philosophy of herbal medicine to his upbringing in Wisconsin. "My father left the farm to go to medical school," recalls Lee. "I guess I turned to philosophy and theology to *escape* medical school and wind up in the herb movement." Upon acquiring his Ph.D. in philosophy at Harvard, Lee embarked on a teaching career that led him from Harvard to MIT, Brandeis, and then out west, to the University of California, Santa Cruz.

Currently, Lee is Dean of the Platonic Academy for Herbal Studies in Santa Cruz and an activist in establishing a professional training center for herbalists. The center's purpose is to recruit and train for the World Health Organization's goal to deliver "Health to All" by the year 2000 through the promotion of herbal medicine.

Paul Lee

The herb renaissance is upon us. It is a renaissance marking a rediscovery and a rebirth of traditional medicine. All you have to do is look at the growth pattern of any herb company in the country or take account of corporations in the food industry bringing out herbal lines, from Lipton tea to Celestial Seasonings. We can look forward to the most intense interest in the field of herbology, medical botany, pharmacognosy, and the history of medicine, when herbs were the main reference point for illness and disease.

This interest is a heartfelt need for roots. Industrial society is a world "above" the given world of nature and therefore it lacks vital roots. We mean to find the roots again. People are going back to natural things, eschewing synthetics—wanting to wear natural fiber clothing, for example. *Vitalism* has returned in the reaffirmation of the qualitative distinction between natural and synthetic.

It has taken roughly a century and a half—from 1828 to the present—for a certain trend, known in the textbooks as *physicalism*, to abate. In the textbooks I've read in the philosophy of science and the history of science, that date, 1828—and the experiment of Wöhler—is designated as marking the defeat of vitalism. By artificially synthesizing urea, Wöhler made urea without a kidney. All at once the

Paul Lee
Santa Cruz, California

distinction between organic and inorganic, natural and synthetic, genuine and counterfeit, broke down. From then on, no vitalist could argue for a "life force" distinguishing organic entities from inorganic ones. If they're chemically identical, what then is the "life force"?

But by 1970 and the Earth Day movement, combined with the renewed interest in ecology and environmentalism, people began to redefine and examine anew their vitalist roots. The task of the herbal renaissance should be to rediscover this tradition and to resummon the powers latent in the unity of mythic figures and plant references. Our herbal roots date back to Grecian times.

Artemis, for example, marks the starting point in herbal lore. Goddess of the wild, her name stands for the artemisias or wormwoods. Achilles is the patron of achillea or yarrows. Chiron the Centaur is the patron of the centauries or medicinal gentians, and Asclepius is the patron of the ascelpiads or milkweeds.

It was to Chiron the Centaur, the horse-man, that the heroes of Greece were sent for their initial instruction in the properties of herbs and their identification. Through his students, the lore was passed on to others. Chiron was the teacher of Achilles and Asclepius, the Greek god of healing, whose sanctuaries became the centers of medical healing through generations of priest-physicians known as the Asclepiads.

In Paul Tillich's book, *The Courage To Be*, he mentions *thymós*, the ancient Greek word which means courage or vitality. Later, when I learned the *thymus* gland and the herb *thyme* were derivative words, I began to acquaint myself with whatever I could find on both. What I have learned in the meanwhile could fill a book.

There is an herb code in the immune memory of DNA. This formulation came to me when I thought through the thyme-thymus connection and affinity between herbology, immunology, and molecular biology (DNA). There is

a genetic transmission of an herbal program in our immune memories. The herb renaissance is devoted to restoring this memory program after a generation or more of
immune amnesia.

Thyme is a germicidal or disinfectant; that is, it kills
germs. It's good for common colds and coughs. The oil of
thyme, thymol, is especially used in cough medicines as a
standard ingredient and in Listerine and Absorbine, Jr. As
a disinfectant, it's superb. Puerto Rico was actually rid of
hookworm by an American doctor using thymol at the
turn of the century. Due to its antiseptic action, thyme has
as broad a product diversification as any herb in the
world.

But, of course, for me, it all started with Tillich. Tillich
greatly influenced me and does to this day. All of the
problems in conceptual formulation and theoretical elab-
oration I once struggled with as a student of theology and
philosophy, I see now in a new light as a result of the
herbal renaissance. When I first went to Harvard, it was
principally to study with Paul Tillich. My father left the
farm to go to medical school. I guess I turned to philosophy and theology to *escape* medical school and wind up in
the herb movement.

I taught at Harvard for about seven years, then MIT for
three. I was Protestant chaplain at Brandeis University for
two years while I was teaching at MIT. Then I moved here
to the University of California, Santa Cruz, where I taught
for seven years.

The big thing at the university at Santa Cruz was starting a garden with Alan Chadwick which could be thought
of as "Findhorn West." My own direct link with herbs
began by virtue of this project and my friendship with Alan.
I was teaching philosophy, religious studies and the history
of consciousness when I had an impulse to begin a garden.

I had a teacher at Harvard Divinity School, George Hun-
ston Williams, who wrote a book called *Wilderness and*

Paradise, which is a tracing of the garden and the desert in the Biblical tradition. The second half of the book is on the idea of the university. He historically documents his thesis that men and women went out from our East Coast into the wilderness to plant a garden which would then be the center for a school of higher education, reenacting the Biblical themes. A seminary, I suppose. I helped him with this book. That's one source I can remember which really affected me.

Also, there was this great ranch landscape and the institutional imposition of the university on it. They had designed the campus to accommodate 27,500 students and 16,000 parking lots. I felt there was a need for roots. A garden seemed the most appropriate means to give that sense.

We began to look for a garden site on campus. Then one day Countess Freya von Möltke came to lunch. She's the widow of Count von Möltke, who died in the German resistance movement in World War II. She had heard about my garden idea. And she had a friend, Alan Chadwick, on his way for a visit. I met him the first day he arrived in Santa Cruz. She said, "He'll do your garden for you," and I said, "Thank you, Countess." He agreed.

Chadwick practiced biodynamics and was inspired by Rudolf Steiner, the founder of biodynamic horticulture, in his youth, but he didn't say a word about Steiner until the garden was well developed and highly acclaimed. The garden had a great influence in California. It changed *Sunset Magazine*'s orientation to organic gardening. Then, after the Earth Day movement in 1970, Chadwick began to reveal what his sources were, through Steiner back to Goethe.

I started to study those intensively and I put together a whole sketch on what I call the physicalist-vitalist debate—that conflict in the sciences that goes back to 1828. I started to understand why things were as bleak as they were when Chadwick came, as though he were designated to replant the vital roots of existence in the late stage of the self-destruction of industrial technocracy. There was a "conspiracy of silence," so to speak, on Steiner's life and work in higher education. Obviously, it was because the physicalists had taken over so completely—you couldn't defend the vitalist position within the university system. If you wanted to, it meant you were out. Maybe you could wind up with the booby prize of being called a naturalist. But there was no status for that within the university system.

Through Chadwick, I came to understand what it meant to replant the vital roots of existence in industrial society. Chadwick knew his job. He had a terrific draw on students. They were magnetized to the garden. And every inch of the way, he led the students through the steps of gardening. How to pick up a spade. How to double dig. Every step, from the most preliminary and inductory on through to the nurturing of vital roots. He worked 15 to 18 hours a day, seven days a week, for some two to three years, before he was persuaded to take a weekend off.

I was amazed at the historical forces that were juxtaposed by virtue of Chadwick coming to the campus and going through this enormous work dynamic that he manifested. E. F. Schumacher, just before his death, said that the only man he knew who could make a great contribution to the solution of the world's food problem was Alan Chadwick and, for Chadwick, herbs were medicinal foods and the secret center of every garden.

The director general of the World Health Organization has called for health care for everyone in the world by the year 2000. He states explicitly that without the help of herbalists worldwide, the goal will be impossible to attain. It's a splendid vision—the thought of delivering health care to everyone. America is unique in having lost touch with traditional herbal medicine. Three-quarters to four-fifths of the health care delivery in the world is herbal.

We'll have to work the hardest to catch up. As this happens, the all-important question for the herb renaissance will be once again—"What's the difference between a chemically synthesized drug and one that's been extracted from a plant?" Or, to put it simply, what's the difference between the organic and the synthetic? It's a critical point.

My dream has been to begin a professional training center for students who want a career in herbal medicine and health care. Thanks to a generous grant from a friend of mine, we were able to begin instruction in 1982, as the first professional training center for herbalists in the U.S. When you look at the national picture, it is a remarkable prospect—where is the college, university, medical school, nursing school, pharmacy school, or nutrition school that teaches a course on medicinal herbs? This situation will soon change, given the intense consumer interest in herbs and what they can contribute to health care.

We intend to train an army of healers devoted to the restoration of the botanical basis of health care as a moral equivalent of war. We are on the way. The route is clear to the replanting of the vital roots. This rebirth of the memory of what nature has to offer is the herb renaissance.

At age 17, *Steven Foster* signed a high school independent study form and set off to find out all he could about Shakers. One thing led to another. First Foster started spending weekends with the Sabbathday Lake, Maine, Shakers, then a few days at a time, then five or six days, and finally, after about a year, he moved in.

For four years, Foster lived and worked within the community. By the time he was ready to leave, he had learned about 200 Shaker songs and acquired an encyclopedic knowledge of Shaker herbalism. Along the way, he had helped develop the contemporary Shaker herb industry, a national mail order business using high quality packaging, fashioned after the Shaker herb tradition of the nineteenth century.

Steven Foster

I see myself as an information person. I collect as much information on herbs as possible, and I try to keep that information flowing. I believe that all information is universal and it should be shared with anyone who's interested.

Now there are two different types: we might call them information and knowledge. On one hand, we have information—something we can read in a book or memorize. On the other hand we have knowledge—something that's actually a part of our being, gained through experience. I call that real knowledge.

A great deal of herb knowledge at this point is simply information. We read from various books on herbs that this herb is good for one thing or another. We read that parsley is a biennial and can be grown from seed, and then we try and grow it from seed and maybe find it doesn't grow for us. All information from books is simply that. It's information until we use it.

To my way of thinking, that's the big difference between American herbology and the knowledge of Europe, China, or South America. The United States stands alone as the country which can provide all of its people with Western medicine: but, at the same time, it lacks virtually all contact with traditional medicine. American herbology

Steven Foster
Mountain View Arkansas

is at a very primitive level right now. We have a tremendous gap of 80 years or so where we haven't been involved with the experiential use of herbs. And now that we're becoming suddenly interested in herbs again, in healing ourselves and decentralizing food sources, it will probably be much harder for us to regain herbal knowledge than for any other culture because of our loss of a traditional lifestyle. It's as if we have no traditions in this country. We're empty souls in respect to our traditions. We don't have elders who have taught us things for years and years.

The state of today's herbology is backward when compared with American herbology in the nineteenth century, when herbs were available in standardized extract form. You could go into a store and you knew exactly what you were getting. The Shakers, for example, produced vacuum-processed and standardized herbal extracts that the physician could rely on every time he bought. He'd know that a certain extract would be a certain strength, and then he'd know which dosage would be right for his patient.

When I was still in high school, I started working at the Shaker community at Sabbathday Lake, Maine. I had a teacher who had been a guide at the Shaker Museum and he directed me there. He set up an interview for me, and I went there, and two days later started working. On my first day, I was asked to go out and gather some burdock leaves—that was my first actual experience in gathering herbs. Harvesting something, bringing it into a drying attic, and tying it up in bundles to dry—I enjoyed it.

Two or three times a week I'd do something with herbs, either package them for the mail order business that the Shaker commuity had at that time or go out in the fields and harvest herbs. Later on, I became immersed in the effort to revitalize the community's herb industry, and I learned a great deal about their history. The Shakers were the first to develop a commercial herb business in this country. Actually, the earliest records of herbs being gathered by the Shakers and sold is the year 1799.

But first of all, before we get to the Shakers, we should understand that there was a big movement in the late eighteenth and early nineteenth centuries to establish herbal medicine in this country as opposed to allopathic medicine. Various sectarian groups of medical practitioners were evolving on different levels. For instance, you could find the Thomsonian physicians (the followers of Samuel Thomson), the botanic-eclectic physicians (who followed Wooster Beach), and then there were the homeopaths. The homeopaths followed the principles set forth by Samuel Hahnemann in the late eighteenth century, but that movement didn't really get going in this country until about the 1840s or so.

Whatever the impetus, there was a strong interest in producing herbs and a strong interest in gathering information on the indigenous native American plants. In 1799, a major essay was delivered before the Philadelphia College of Pharmacy called "An Essay Towards the Materia Medica of the U.S.," by Benjamin Smith Barton. At this time, the medical profession was trying to find a way to use plants the Indians used instead of importing all of their herbs from Europe. They looked to Barton, since he was one of the prominent botanists in the U.S. What they discovered was that the Indians' medicine really worked, so they started taking a serious look at native North American herbs.

At this same time the followers of Samuel Thomson were using a combination of native American herbs and European plants, showing people how they could become their own physicians. They wanted people to know that they could treat themselves with the plants that grew around them. Any man who could gather his own food could just as easily go out and gather his own medicines.

So, anyway, there were the Thomsonians and the bo-tanic-eclectic physicians with the homeopaths coming along a bit later. And it's because of these movements that the Shakers got into the commerical herb business. At first, they just gathered herbs for use within their own communities. They had nurse shops in each community where nurses would treat the sick. Pretty soon they developed a rich tradition of herbal recipes and techniques for healing. For example, there's a thing that's fairly popular among modern herbal neophytes called cleansing. Well, the Shakers and other early Americans would cleanse themselves in the springtime with various teas, like dandelion root, burdock root, or sassafras. And one aspect of cleansing was "puking," and the Shakers had concoctions called pukes. Every spring, you'd formulate the puke, take it, and let everything go. That would mark the start of a new spring.

One misconception that people often have about the Shakers is that they're a stagnant fragment of the nineteenth century. I think this is because most of the books about Shakers deal with the time before 1850 or so. People see these old engravings of Shaker furniture from the 1820s or see them dancing and think that's what the Shakers are all about. But, in fact, the Shakers are very progressive and move with the times. Just as in our society we've fallen out of the use of natural medicines, gathering our own herbs and using them for our own purposes, so it is in the Shaker tradition. However, stronger remnants remain with the Shakers than in general society.

The widespread use of herbs started to decline about 100 years ago—in the 1870s and 1880s—and became completely phased out around the 1920s. The history of the Shaker herb industry exemplifies the birth, the peak, and the decline of the whole botanic medicine movement in the U.S. If we look at the timeline: in the 1790s, the Shakers sell their first herbs, in the 1820s herbs become a big business for them as they sell their supplies to both the allopathic and botanic physicians, and then, in the late nineteenth century, the decline sets in.

In their heyday, the Shakers' physic gardens, as they were called—which were herb gardens—would make use of up to 150 acres. On the one hand, the Shakers supplied crude opium from their poppy plants to the allopathic physicians, and on the other, they supplied lobelia—the main herb of the Thomsonians—to the Thomsonian physicians. They bridged both movements in supplying high quality herbs. In the pharmaceutical company catalogs there were certain Shaker herbs and patent medicines, whereas in the botanic suppliers' catalogs there was a very different line of Shaker medicines.

By the late nineteenth century, the Shaker herb industry evolved into a "patent medicine" business. They sold such products as Shaker anodyne, Shakers' fluid extract of English valerian, and syrup of sarsaparilla, a popular tonic. There were lots of tonics on the market and lots of companies which, unlike the Shakers, produced products with absolutely no effects—just sugar and syrup. It was at this time that Coca-Cola first appeared, including extracts from the leaves of the coca plant, but then the Pure Food and Drug Act of 1906 came along, and it took the zip out of Coca-Cola and put many patent medicine companies out of business. Synthetics start coming around the 1880s and 1890s and you see more pure alkaloids, more pure extracts, rather than crude plant products coming into the *materia medica* of the allopathic physicians.

Today, the people at the Shaker village go to doctors like most people do, there's nothing in their philosophy that prevents that. Still, herbs are sometimes used within the community. Many of the sisters remember when herbs were used in their childhood, they remember the pots of motherwort or lemon balm tea always at the back of the stove. One sister there, Sister Mildred—a saint in her own right—can remember when she was a child in the community, the only thing they took for chicken pox was catnip tea.

For the last three or four generations, Shakers have become removed from the domestic use of medicinal herbs. It's just like when I go and speak at the senior citizen centers, about half of the people will come up to me afterwards and say, "I can remember my grandmother using those herbs, but we don't use those things anymore. Now we use prescription drugs."

The pattern of the Shaker community is, in that way, just like the rest of society. Today, here in the U.S., we have one type of medicine—Western, or allopathic. But there are virtually as many medical systems as there are cultures in various parts of the world. What I'd really like to see someday is small herb farms springing up throughout the country to supply local markets. What's needed are studies to show the small farmer how he can grow herbs as a cash crop—drying them with solar energy and perhaps handling up to a thousand pounds of fresh herbs daily. We need simple and inexpensive techniques to process the herbs right on the farm, to keep them fresh. And we have to develop intensive and efficient labor methods which will allow us to compete with other countries. That is one of my dreams, and it's a dream that is inspired by my work with the Shakers. Even today, a great deal of the Shaker herb information is in the form of genuine knowledge, it's based on the experience of a traditional lifestyle.

After reading scores of books on herbs, diet, and health, *"Herbal" Ed Smith* embarked for the Amazon jungle. There he studied with the *curanderos* and the old herb women. Eventually he had the opportunity to run a small clinic in Guatemala, set up primarily for treating sick vagabonding Americans. Persons with hepatitis, fevers, dysentery, and skin rashes would show up on his doorstep. But for Smith, "this was an incredible experience, and, of course, I wouldn't have been able to do it in the United States."

Studying botanical pharmacy, *materia medica*, and therapeutics at the Harvard Medical School and botanical libraries, as well as studying folk medicine with the *curanderos* of South America, has enabled Smith to learn the herbal roots of two different worlds. Today, he seeks a balance between overly simplistic herb knowledge on the one hand and the overly sophisticated on the other.

"Herbal" Ed Smith

Back in the early 1970s, when I first looked into it, there weren't too many people teaching herbs. I talked to as many people as I could, burned the midnight oil, and read just about every herb book I could get my hands on. Every time a new one would come out, I'd buy it. Then I started collecting old pharmacy books and old *materia medicas.* Mostly, I got books that were written around the early 1900s, when herbology was still being practiced in a professional way.

A lot of those books are incredible textbooks. They're really very difficult books to find, but they're just gold mines of information when you can find them. They were written by medical doctors who used herbs in thousands of cases. I have a 1925 catalog here in my library from Lilly Drug Company which lists literally hundreds of different herbal preparations—everything from crude botanicals all the way up to fluid extracts, herb tinctures, and prepared poultice mixtures. Whatever you could pretty much imagine, they sold. You could buy these at any drugstore in any city in the U.S.

You could buy a tincture of lobelia or a fluid extract of goldenseal or tincture of marijuana or black cohosh or almost any herb you could name. They were being made and used by medical professionals. By the early 1900s,

"Herbal" Ed Smith
Williams, Oregon

medical doctors were still using herbs in their offices and hospitals, and firms like Parke-Davis and Lilly were marketing them.

So what happened? As you read the books that were written during this time, you'll see that by 1930 a lot of herbs started fading away from the professional books, and they would be replaced by more chemical drugs—especially in the '30s and '40s, with the advent of modern chemistry and the petroleum industry. They started taking petroleum and making drugs out of it. Herbs became less and less common and more and more disfavored by the doctors. In old editions of the *U.S. Dispensatory*, which is about the oldest pharmacy book in the United States, they rave about the use of herbs. Then you read the more modern edition in the '30s and '40s and you see a lot of pessimism coming in when they start to put herbs down. Today, in the modern *U.S. Pharmacopoeia* and the *National Formulary*, there are probably fewer than half a dozen herb tinctures and extracts that are "official." In the 1890s, there were hundreds. They just faded away.

We're not really that far from it in terms of our heritage. Here I'm talking about the professional level. It's always been happening on a folk level. The old grandmas who nursed the kids with sweat packs and herbs for measles, mumps, and fevers. That didn't fade quite so quickly but with the Second World War, even that started fading. With the decentralization of the family in America, the daughter no longer learned from her grandmother because her grandmother was living somewhere else. A lot of our knowledge just got left behind with the war. What used to be common knowledge—simple things like onion poultices, mustard plasters, enemas, different herbal concoctions—these things were completely lost and not passed on to the families. When I did a workshop in Washington, a 95-year-old woman was in my class. Quite frankly, I probably learned as much about herbs from her as anybody else in the class learned from me. She had done it. She had used the herbs.

That's one reason I finally went to South America to learn about herbs. Probably what I was experiencing in South America in the early 1970s was pretty much what happened in this country in the 1800s. You can go to a market anywhere in South America, and the people are selling herbs, even in the major cities like Bogota—which is a big city with skyscrapers, 747s landing, and cars zipping around. And a lot of these herbs are fresh-picked that morning by the herb women. You'll find some of the more displaced Amazonian Indians living in Bogota—somewhat pitiful to watch—and they're selling herbs that they've gathered from the Amazon jungle. And, of course, they're not only selling herbs but they're giving advice on how to use them. They've got everything, everything from different herbs for poisonous bites, various sicknesses, herbs for unfaithful husbands, love charms, and a lot of other things. Of course, some of this is probably superstition, but most of it is very valid.

All in all, I spent a period of several years—a lot of winters—in South America. I was working through a degree program at a University Without Walls and getting the G.I. Bill for college credit. Specifically, I went in a very structured sort of way to look for and study with herbalists. I went to Guatemala and studied for three months there in a Seventh-day Adventist medical missionary school called Instituto Naturalista. I also worked in their clinics, where we treated sick people with herbs, hydrotherapy, massage, diet, etc. Later on, I set up my own clinic on Lake Atitlán, where I treated a lot of wandering American travelers who were suffering with what I called the "Gringo Blues"—maladies incurred in a tropical environment, like typhoid fever, dysentery, hepatitis, and intestinal worms. I had a small house which I lived in and another larger house which I used as a clinic.

In my herbal studies in South America, I mainly just moved around different parts of the Amazon jungle, different oil towns and river villages, just asking for people who were *curanderos*. And, of course, I found a lot of people who claimed to be *curanderos*. It was kind of a frustrating search because the jungle itself was very difficult to live in, and I was trying to find somebody I felt was really genuine and who was truly carrying on the old traditions.

Eventually, I came across this man's name from several different people—Don Salvador. I was able to find out approximately where he lived, but I had to catch a ride on a canoe going down river. The man who gave me the ride turned out to be his son—that was quite a coincidence! Anyway, I just went in and spent some time with this man.

While I was there, he showed me many different kinds of herb uses. We also partook of a plant, a hallucinogen, that they used called yagé. It's also called *Banisteriopsis caapi*, the Latin name for it. It's a vine that grows in the jungle. He would administer that and also, of course, do different rituals—dancing, songs, and chants. They use the plant there for everything from schizophrenia to diabetes to colitis, snake bites, hepatitis, whatever. Because it's so strong, and very bitter tasting, it causes a lot of vomiting. But it's a great cleanser for the liver and gallbladder.

The basis of his whole practice, including his involvement with the hallucinogens—which is indigenous to all the *curanderos* in the Amazon area—is to create a lot of visions.

Because Don Salvador has taken the yagé so many times, his control over the visions is very powerful, and he "sees" much more than the average person. This is how he is able to "diagnose" his patients and find the appropriate remedy.

Although I did gain specific knowledge about the use of

medicinal plants from Don Salvador, I do feel that my most meaningful lessons were learned through taking the yagé and my participation in the yagé healing ceremony. It was here that I started to understand what shamanistic healing is about—you can't just treat the body, you have to treat the being that lives inside the body.

When you go into the primitive areas of South America, you find herbology is a major part of people's lives. A lot of people don't have access to medicines—depending upon how far they're isolated in the jungle—but they do have *curanderos*. In our country, medical doctors play a major role in the community. Well, there it's the herbalist who plays the major role. If you talk about herbs to a well-educated lawyer or a government official in South America, they don't laugh at you. They may not use them, but they don't laugh. They'll say, I know, my mother uses them and they work. Here, of course, a lot of people think you're crazy. They don't understand them at all. But that's just because they've lost touch with their historical roots.

Of course, now we're experiencing an herb renaissance—well, not just an herb renaissance, but a whole natural healing renaissance. A lot of these skills are being re-learned through books, and the young people are learning from the old people. In the course of my travels in South America, I built up a cross-reference chart which I carried around with me. I would have the common American names with the common Spanish names and the inter-relating Latin name. A lot of times I discovered that they used the same herbs which we used in American folk medicine. To me it was always very exciting to see a common herb used in the same way by herbalists in two totally different places and in two totally different times. Plantain is one of those herbs. Everybody in South America knows plantain. They use it for cuts, burns, snake bites, and insect bites. They also know it's good for the liver. You can look in any herb book in the United States under plantain and locate the exact same uses.

To me, when I see a correlation like that, matching up in two totally different cultures, there's some truth there. That's when you start to find out what herbs are all about, and your search really starts to come alive.

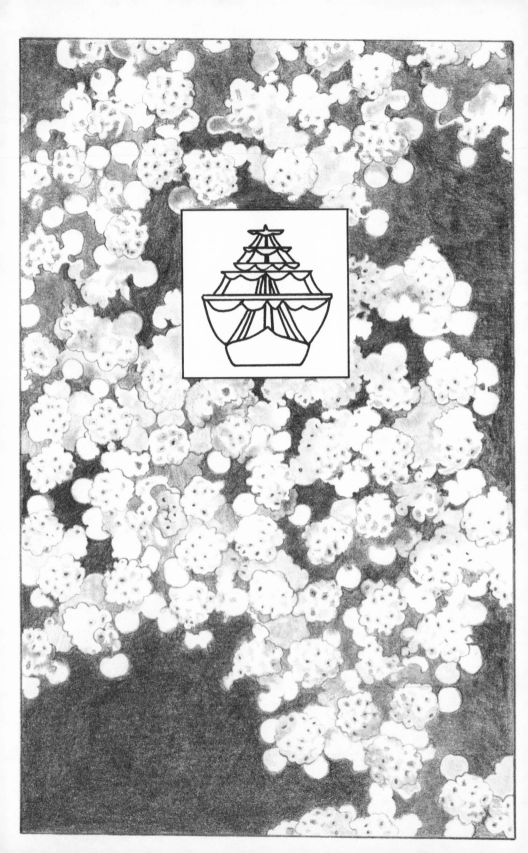

CHAPTER TWO

Seeds

In AMERICA our herbal seeds have been scattered to the winds. As the immigrant populations melted into the mainstream, virtually all of our imported traditions vanished. German settlements were swallowed by big cities and Chinatowns turned into tourist attractions.

Today, the strongest unbroken herbal links may be found among the Chinese and Native Americans, as well as among the folk cultures of the American Southeast. Occasionally, as in the case of Ayurvedic medicine from India, a new seed appears on our shores, awaiting our nourishment and understanding of a system that dates to the beginnings of recorded history.

When the first settlers arrived in this country, they found that the American Indians had evolved an effective medical system based on the use of wild herbs, roots, and barks. Indian herbs such as butternut bark, bloodroot, slippery elm, and pokeberry soon found a place in the white man's medicine chest, right beside the Old World's saffron, tansy, pennyroyal, sorrel, and garlic.

No doubt the most significant of the Indian remedies was Peruvian bark, which served as a popular treatment for malaria. Although the bark's active ingredient,

47

quinine, makes up only about 2 to 5 percent of the crude bark, great quantities were consumed by U.S. soldiers in the early days to ward off the disease. By about 1820, quinine was isolated from Peruvian bark, and soon after, its use as a malaria cure spread throughout the continent. Today, tonic or quinine water offers a modern-day reminder of the original potion.

Another popular Indian remedy, willow bark (which contains salicin), is now synthetically produced as salicylic acid and is the effective ingredient in aspirin.

The Indians represented in Chapter Two tell of the sacred rites and remedies passed down within the tribal cultures. *Sun Bear* and *Wabun, Keetoowah,* and *Rolling Thunder* offer differing perspectives, but their respect for Mother Earth is universal. In their accounts one finds tales of vision quests and powerful herbs, mixed with reports on our earliest, and oft-forgotten, chapters of American history.

Although the first major impact of Chinese medicine in this country came much later, roughly coinciding with the early bustle of the Gold Rush, fears and superstitions immediately drew a tight curtain around the rich Chinese traditions. Only recently have our medical scientists been willing to accept acupuncture and herbal treatments as valuable adjuncts to allopathic medicine.

In the attempt to synthesize Eastern and Western medical techniques, China provides an intriguing model. Following Mao Tse-tung's call in the mid-1950s to "make the past serve the present," pharmaceutical and medical research workers embarked on a program to uncover the scientific basis of the country's age-old herbal treatments. Their findings are still incomplete, but already some 4,000 of the country's estimated 5,000 medicinal herbs have been subjected to at least preliminary studies.

China's push is to make a nation of healthy people, explains *Nam Singh.* "You see," he notes, "if you allow society to become full of sick people, you're not very strong as a nation. And China wants to be very strong." In the People's Republic of China, doctors trained in Western medicine use herbal preparations and other related means of prevention according to the individual patient's needs and wishes. Given the choice, roughly 70 percent of appendicitis patients at one hospital chose herbal treatment. But when infection enters into the picture, doctors are quick to suggest antibiotics and surgery.

In similar manner, India today unites ancient and new. Recent efforts have kindled widespread respect for what is the oldest recorded system of medicine in the world. Ayurvedic instruction, passed from Indian masters to their disciples, predates even Chinese medicine. Over the millenia, Indian scriptures have detailed such subjects as pediatrics, obstetrics, plastic surgery, and internal medicine. "Such a treasure of science is stored in the Vedas," remarks *Dr. Vasant Lad*, "that scientists everywhere must open their eyes without prejudice."

In our own country, little written documentation exists for our grassroots herbal practices. Yet, in the folk cultures of the Southeastern states, such wisdom is readily available to those who take the opportunity to listen to the old-timers. *Billy Joe Tatum* and her physician husband have collected literally thousands of home herbal recipes from their neighbors, a project that has taken more than 25 years of work and understanding. "Mountain people will treat you as an equal only if you really are equal," explains Billy Joe. "Honesty is what they look for."

Tommie Bass of Leesburg, Alabama, is one of those who has opened his doors to the curious. "I'm glad to answer any question that I know I can answer truthfully," comments Bass. "But I don't answer if I don't know."

When we look in distant corners and consult with people who may have come from far-off lands, we find that our herbal seeds are still plentiful. To grow, they require only an open ear, a receptive heart, and understanding.

Keetoowah is a Cherokee medicine man born in Tahlequah, Oklahoma, who now lives in a Santa Rosa, California, suburb. A heavy-set man with a hearty laugh, Keetoowah smokes one pack of cigarettes per day—one of the consequences, he says, of being a medicine man. Medicine men are often paid in tobacco, which is a powerful and sacred medicine.

As a boy, Keetoowah was taught the Indian ways by his mother. Three vision quests followed and provided Keetoowah with knowledge of his life's work.

As a medicine man, Keetoowah keeps in touch with other medicine people such as Grandfather Semu and Rolling Thunder. "Each one does something a little better than someone else does," explains Keetoowah. "I'll refer you to them if you have a problem I can't handle."

Keetoowah

I've known since I was about five years old that there were
a lot of things that were different about me. We all have
the same innate abilities and powers. In that respect, I'm
nothing special. Just another person made out of flesh,
blood, and bone like other people. It's just that I've become aware of the things that I could do and certain things
that have happened to me.

I'm a half-breed Cherokee from Tahlequah, Oklahoma,
but didn't really grow up anywhere. I left Tahlequah
when I was four years old, adopted by wealthy white
parents. Lots of money, but little love and affection. They
used to ask me, do you need another hundred? Here it is.
Of course, I got some help, but most of all I wanted knowledge, more than anything else. I wanted to know. I
wanted to find out the truth.

I'd spend summers with my grandparents. My mother
taught me; she made me learn, repeat the lesson over and
over and over. The inflection, pronunciation—I had to
learn all of the Cherokee rituals, traditions, and ceremonies. Then grandmother used to rap one of those great
big thimbles, like you used to wear, right on top of my
head when I got something wrong. You learn in self-
defense! My mother and father were both part Cherokee—
half Cherokee and half "savage." We've been that way for

51

Keetoowah
Santa Rosa, California

at least seven generations—half-breeds. Of course, I'm not sure we're a minority any longer. Almost everyone I talk to is part Cherokee or part Arapahoe or something. There are so many tribes.

I went on a vision quest three different times. They all came out more or less the same. The first time I was nine, then twelve, then finally about sixteen. I've never been more than three days on a vision quest. Some people stay two or three weeks but that's murder—no food, no water, or anything—just naked on top of a mountain somewhere. It's rough, but it never took me more than three days.

When you come down, you need an interpreter. A person has to go to a medicine person. When he's sick, even a medicine person doesn't say, "I'm sick and I know what's wrong with me, and I'll drink some of this and get rid of it." He can't do that. I cannot heal myself and I won't even try. I have to ask someone else. When you aren't personally involved you can see more clearly—it's like watching a checker game—you can see a move where neither player can figure it.

All three vision quests meant the same thing. But that meaning we don't reveal. There are also other answers too. In a vision quest, you will get one answer, but there are also other answers. And if I need to, I can tell you I don't know the answer. I'm not ashamed of it. Go find somebody that does. Go ask Semu or Rolling Thunder. I'll refer you to them if you have a problem I can't handle. We specialize, more or less. There are some things that doctors can do that medicine men can't do. Like a double hernia or a displaced vertebra. That may take surgery. That may be the only way to fix it.

Each one does something a little better than someone else does. When we realize that, we can neglect some of the things that we can't do so well. Everything I do, I do extremely well. That's not bragging. It just makes sense to me. If you can't do it, forget it. Do something you can do. Keep it simple.

You can't be a medicine person just because you want to, that's one thing I'm sure of. I've had people come here trying to become a medicine person. There was a young man here last week. He felt the call, he felt the urge, he wanted to teach, to be a healer. He didn't have a very good chance of doing it. I don't know a medicine person who wants to be one.

Books and teachers are plentiful. Teachers aren't hard to find, and they can tell you that senna leaves are a laxative and rose hips have vitamin C. All this information is very, very available, but you can only go so far with it. With medicine people there is something more. I can't explain it. I wish I could.

Medicine persons are usually very uneducated—what we call educated. But they can look at a plant and say, "I don't know the name of it, I don't know what you would call it, but this is what it's good for." Take something like cancer of the uterus. For two cases maybe it's white pond lily root; for the next maybe it's something completely different. We're all individuals, and there is a slight difference in each of us. What makes one person sick will cure the other.

Herbs have vibrations; they give off sounds and they have feelings. If it were not for the plants, we wouldn't be here. We're "inhaling" what they're putting out. You feel different in the forest. I don't care how sensitive or insensitive you are. You feel different. You walk through the giant redwoods and feel peaceful. Those redwoods are not making much of a disturbance. They're not fighting each other. They're not aggressive. The little plants don't put up much resistance, but that doesn't mean they don't "cry out." Put a lie detector on a tomato and then threaten it. That tomato screams in a way that can be seen on a piece of graph paper. Plants have feelings. A prerequisite for all medicine people is that they have respect for all living things.

I always gather herbs in the daytime and I always make an offering. You have to pay for everything—one way or the other. The way I gather sage illustrates that. We use a lot of sage. There are several different kinds, and we use the one that's most convenient. If I happen to be going through the desert and it's convenient, I just stop the car and walk a half mile off the road and start picking. I'm grateful for the sage. I'm grateful that people have taught me what I can do with it and what it's used for. It costs me only a pinch or two of tobacco. That would be an offering.

Tobacco is a very, very powerful medicine. It is sacred. Some readers may remember the old G.I. trick. When you wanted to get on sick call, you checked in with the nurse and just wet a cigarette and put it in your armpit for a few minutes. The nurse took your temperature and said, "Get this man in the hospital. He's got a 103 or 104 fever." There was nothing wrong with you, but you did have the fever. Well, sometimes we need a fever to burn off and kill germs, for example. Sometimes you need to be hot inside. But you don't have to take the heat inside of you.

In using the medicine pipe and things like that, you never inhale. That smoke and heat shouldn't be in your lungs. The smoke should go up and carry a message to the Creator.

Marijuana is a good medicine. It's not meant to get high on for recreation. It's not for that purpose. If I am in extreme pain (and I've done this), I get in bed and take a quantity that would make a cigarette or two. It tastes green so I chew it up and drink water or milk or something and wash it all down. I don't get high. I just let the muscles relax. Lie back and sleep, and the next morning, I'm hungry and raring to go. That's using medicine the way it's meant to be used. Nature has a tendency to balance.

When you give medicine people tobacco, it's because

it's sacred. We give it as an offering. Hold it in the hand. Every morning at sunrise, first to the east, south, west, north, Sun, and Mother Earth. I do something to earn that tobacco, but it's much better to throw that tobacco down as an offering than to throw down a dollar. If I drop a silver dollar on the ground and somebody comes along and sees it, it doesn't go where I want it to. But if I throw a pinch or two of tobacco on the ground, no one's going to come along accidentally, find it, pick it up, and smoke it. It is protection for the plants for one thing. An insecticide. A repellent. Insects live by rules, too. Some people call it cosmic law.

There's only one thing on this planet that I'm afraid of and that's me. I know what I'm capable of, and I have to explain things clearly, such as that you're to leave poisons alone, or that you're not to take herbs or medicines unless you know what you're doing. If you're not sure of anything at any time, back up. Retreat. I wouldn't give or recommend a medicine I haven't used on myself.

The simplest way to find out about herbs is to go out and talk to them on a one-to-one basis. You don't go down the street and tip your hat and say, "Hi, Mr. Tree, Mrs. Tree." They're going to lock you up if you do. Put it in your "computer" and use a little judgment. Go out by yourself, look around and be certain no one's watching you. Then sit down and talk to an herb plant. You won't get any reaction for a while. But keep on—believe me, you will.

For every disease of mankind, I believe there is a plant that can cure it. I believe there is nothing herbs can't cure. There are thousands and thousands of plants, different species and kinds all over the world. And now we know that those plants have feelings. Well, the Indians have known that since the beginning.

The Indians were put in a special place for a reason—we

are guardians and custodians of the earth, this part of the earth. When I travel, I find a witch doctor or medicine person or somebody equivalent and find out how he does his work. If I go to Rolling Thunder's up in Nevada and say, "Why do you do the ceremony to the east, the north, the south, and the west? You know, at home, we go sun-wise, east, south, west, north, Sun, and Mother Earth." He just grins and says, "This is Shoshone country. This place was set aside for Shoshones. Let's do it like they do it." In Pomo country I ask the Pomo medicine lady, "What did you burn and what are the names of the herbs and where did you get them?" She uses horsetail tea and things like that—we don't have them in Oklahoma.

I have lived more than 60 years and have learned a lot of things not to do. I've been to school all over the world in just about every way you can "go to school." Does it work, or doesn't it? I want to find out the truth of it. And because I have done all this I probably know a little more than most other people. So people come and ask me. This makes me a chief or medicine person? It just happens that I am one who wants to know. I have a grandson, another Keetoowah. He's going to start in where I finish. He's right in line. He's going to take my place and keep going. We're finding new things all the time. I'm passing them on to him. He'll take all I know and go on with this work.

Rolling Thunder has been an inspiration and a catalyst for many. By some, he has been called an intertribal medicine man, spiritual leader, and philosopher. In his own mind, he doesn't claim to be anything. "All power belongs to the Great Spirit," he says. "I want that clear right now."

Endowed with a simple, yet noble manner, Rolling Thunder puffs calmly on a corncob pipe while telling of the Indians' ways and reminiscing of linkages that have brought him into contact with celebrities such as folk singer Bob Dylan, and various New Age groups.

Rolling Thunder's own community, Meta Tantay, is located on a 262-acre tract in eastern Nevada surrounded by high mountains. There, his followers are developing the land for living in simple ways, raising animals, planting crops, and gathering herbs.

Rolling Thunder

I've been among many different people. I've learned to dress in different ways. I've come to know the white man and the Chinese. But sometimes those people didn't know who I was or why I was there. I have friends everywhere and among all races. Twenty years ago, I couldn't say that.

About 15 years ago, two stars changed position in the sky. Many of us were watching it. When those two stars changed position, the prophecies told us we no longer had to be intimidated. We could stand up and meet with other people, and we were to travel all over the world and find our brothers and sisters. Those sons of medicine men and chiefs who were born light-complexioned, dressed in business suits and were educated, and they traveled all over the world, through every religion and every country. They had been highly trained to fulfill a purpose. That job has been done, and my "monkey suit," the business suit, is hanging in the closet with dust all over it. That job is done—I may never have to wear it again. I hope not. I don't like it.

Many people say I'm a medicine man. I don't make any claims; I want that clear right now. All power belongs to the Great Spirit. Yet, some say I am a medicine man. Maybe to them I am. Some say they got well—I fixed their broken backs, or other things. Maybe to them I am a

Rolling Thunder
Meta Tantay, Nevada

medicine man. There are others I know that have said I wasn't, and to them I'm not. It's that simple. People ask me what I do, and I must tell them that I don't do anything at all. I am merely an intermediary between the Great Spirit and the people around me.

I learned my destiny through the events of my early years. You see, I was raised in eastern Oklahoma, in a range of the Ozarks called the Kiamichi Mountains. At about the age of 15, I built my first house, a log cabin with a separate smokehouse and a corral for goats and hogs. I lived alone there for quite a while, and worked about an acre of land with a hoe and a shovel.

Those were rough times, but they taught me a lot about nature and about ways of living in harmony with Mother Earth. I learned how to forage for nuts, berries, and roots in the forest and how to catch fish by setting traps in the water. I also taught myself to recognize all the local woodland plants, although I never got to know many by their English or Latin names. Instead, I made up my own labels for each one, and I learned how to use them for food and medicine.

I always tell people that I'm the worst; I'm not perfect. I've got a lot of hang-ups. I drink coffee and smoke strong tobacco. And some have said that 20 years ago I liked the women. I never want to be considered perfect. I never want to be considered that way, because then someone would get suspicious and they might think I was a politician.

We Indians like people, life, nature, babies, and animals. We've learned to get along with nature. We have a perfect relationship with animals. The wild coyotes don't bother our rabbits and chickens. We've made an agreement with the animals and they respect our Indian religion. Our religion is about life. Our songs are happy, lively songs. That's why we bring our drums along with us. We sing songs about life.

The circle is the emblem of our religion. It's the form of the earth, of the universe. We Indians talk in circles. Everything goes in circles.

Medicine men only tell you so much at a given time. They want you to figure out what they mean for your-selves. Their greatest fear is that they might hurt some-one—an animal or whatever. All the power and energy comes from the Sun and the Great Spirit. The Great Spirit covers everything that has life in it—the rocks, mountains, everything with movement.

Every plant is good for something. I must approach a plant humbly if I intend to take it for medicine. I make an offering and talk to it. And I only take the herb between sunrise and sunset. Mother Earth must be respected. She has life and is a living body just like we are. Some herbs I take on instinct. I may take an herb that has never been there before. But it's what I need and it's waiting there just for me. There are a million herbs and new ones coming on now. You have to learn how to approach plants. If an herbalist pulls an herb from the ground without an offer-ing, his medicine will be weak.

Herbs can also be used as "helpers." I gather my own plants for use in healing ceremonies, but that's not as easy as it may sound. It's necessary to know where and when to look for the plants, and then—once you've located the necessary ones—how to approach them correctly so that they'll yield their special energy to you. When I go out to collect herbs, I can usually *feel* their presence before I actu-ally see the plants. Often they simply appear when—and where—they're needed. In fact, there have been times when I've gathered summer flowers while snow was on the ground, but that sort of thing happens only when the need for the herb is very great.

I'm sure you've noticed that plants usually grow in clumps. Well, that's because they tend to live in families or tribes, just as human beings do. When you want to cut off an herb's leaves or flowers, you should first pay your respects to the chief of the group by making a small offering (I use tobacco, or some item that's of personal value to me). Then you should communicate with the plant and tell it that you're going to take leaves from only a few of its tribal members, and that they're going to be used for a good purpose, for healing.

I never harvest more than half of a medicinal plant's foliage—so it can continue to reproduce—and if I find a stand of herbs that consists of just one or two individuals, I always pass it by. Now I know such precautions sound silly to some people, especially those who think wild plants are nothing more than weeds; but to me they're not weeds, they're living beings and I respect them.

We've got to slow down and learn from Mother Earth. To become a medicine man, you've got to learn to slow down. It takes 20 or 30 years of training to become a medicine man. You must approach the Great Spirit's power and learn respect.

Chief Joseph, one of our great chiefs, looks fierce. Many people look at his picture and think he was a fierce man. He wasn't. The United States Army chased him through parts of Oregon, I think it was, and Idaho and Montana, and he almost made it into Canada. He almost got away. They were chasing him and his whole tribe, and the women and children. They study his tactics at West Point to try to understand how he did it. The main complaint of his own people was that with the soldiers a few miles back he'd see a flower, and he'd have to get off his horse and examine the flower and smell it and look at it. If that's what they call fierce or savage, then we need more such people.

The only real solution, I think, is honesty. The government should be honest with the Indians and begin to observe the treaties originally agreed upon—those documents are still valid. I think that we might be able to reach such a goal with the help of the new generation of young men and women who care about the lot of the native Americans. I really hope that we can bring together our two peoples. That's our goal here at Meta Tantay, where an almost equal mixture of Indians and non-Indians are living together. The name of our desert camp, by the way, means "to go in peace," and that's what we're trying to do.

We Indians—we're the ones who knew how to take care of the Mother Earth, and still do—we know the law of the land and nature. Where we walk, every plant, every rock, every stone, or anything that moves in the forest, we know the meaning of, and we know that these things should be protected instead of destroyed. Peace is the key to health.

In his youth, *Sun Bear* had a vision of a time coming in which his people would be called upon to teach non-native people about changes in the Mother Earth and how to live self-sufficiently in times of stress. Taught by his own visions and people from various tribes and traditions, and by his uncles, Sun Bear suggests, "If you want to be an herbalist, let the earth teach you about the plants."

Wabun wrote for *Life* magazine and lived in New York City before she was introduced to herbs through Sun Bear's teaching. She is deeply concerned about present ways of growing and gathering herbs which fail to respect the Mother Earth.

According to Wabun, a medicine person is a sacred person who approaches healing holistically. Like other medicine men, Sun Bear won't recommend an herb until he has gathered it himself or used it on others.

The Bear Tribe, founded in 1970 by Sun Bear, is a society of Indians and non-Indians whose primary purpose is to teach people to have "a better balance within themselves."

Sun Bear
Spokane, Washington

Sun Bear

Our people were told of certain changes that would come upon the earth. I learned their prophecies and visions, and in my own visions I saw these things too. I was about 15 years old when I first had the vision. It was a powerful dream, not a vision quest. I saw the time coming when native and non-native people would have to come together in love and harmony to learn how to live in balance. Our work now is to try to teach self-sufficiency and unity on the Earth Mother—how to raise food, to build housing, and to know the edible wild plants and herbs. This is our work.

Medicine men come to knowledge in different ways. Some have powerful visions. This might be what gives a person the direction and makes him a medicine man. Others might study with different people. A medicine man knows that he's ready to practice his vision when he can make something happen. He can will it and make it happen. Then it becomes real and the vision goes before him all his life. It sort of pushes him forward. It's something you have to fulfill, you have to follow it. That's what my medicine has been. I couldn't do anything other than what I'm doing.

Our people have a great knowledge of healing. The average medicine man has a knowledge of about 150 different herbs. Some of these are powerful stimulants, even poisons, but used in small amounts they can help cure illness. When we go out to harvest herbs we never take from the first plant of the species. We'll offer a prayer at that plant and then go on to the next one. This has been our way. We feel that the Great Spirit has put upon the Earth Mother a cure for every sickness. It is the way of our people.

We tell of a time when there was an old man who came to the villages. He went to many different villages and the people were afraid of him. They turned him away because he had great sores all over his arms. Finally, he came to a village of the Bear Clan. An elderly lady had a lodge on the outside of the camp, and he came by her door. She said to him, "Grandfather, come on in, and have some soup with me." So he came into her house and she served him soup. She looked and she saw big sores on his arms. She said, "Can I help you with your sickness?" He told her which herbs to gather to treat the sickness. She treated him and he became well.

Immediately after this he got another sickness, and he told her what herbs to gather to cure that sickness. It went like this until he had given her the knowledge of all the sicknesses of mankind at that time. Then he told her that he was a spirit man and had come to bring this gift. Because she had been kind to him, that medicine would be with the Bear Clan and the Chippewas. That's the story of the way medicine has come to us.

After I was 18, I left the Chippewas and started searching for another tribal ground. I left home because I had more to learn, and I knew that I had a responsibility for a larger world focus. So I left and went out to study and travel. I traveled to many other tribes. In the process I learned how to do some of the many things we're doing now. I went to the Omaha Indians and the Winnebagos and lived with them. I learned good things from them. I traveled to the Pimas and Navajos. Primarily it was just sitting and listening and being a part of them, accepting what they had to teach. Although some members of the tribes would go to other tribes, it wasn't a common practice. But people who are looking for a larger knowledge seek it out.

One thing that people have to watch for in the use of herbs is not to become too dogmatic. A lot of people get into something and immediately feel they know all the answers. They've got one part and then proclaim that as the whole core of knowledge.

Today, if someone has a major blood poisoning or infection, and he is about to die, we can't tell him to cleanse himself with herbs. You can't be dogmatic. You have to take responsibility for his life. You work with what's available at the time. If we have to use antibiotics to save someone's life, we do.

But we see a time coming when a lot of people are going to have to know for themselves how to treat various sicknesses. Otherwise they may not survive. With our work, we use burdock, mullein, chamomile, mints, and nettles. All these things come from our local area. We also use alfalfa, comfrey, St. John's wort, and pine needles and quaking aspen. Quaking aspen is very good for the stomach. The inner bark is used for stomachache. It's also good for energy, as a spring tonic herb. We make a tea out of the fir and pine needles, and sometimes we use it as a bath water for people with respiratory and nervous problems.

At this stage of evolution, you sometimes have to use the white man's medicine for the white man's sickness. We accept those things, but we try to keep as healthy as possible. I don't think the medical profession is going to be that readily available for a lot of the sicknesses that are going to be happening. The very thing that is going to save people is a closeness to the land and a balance with the natural forces. There are herbs available within about

50 miles for almost every sickness that can come to you. When the time comes that herbs can't come from some distant land, it will be good to know about those that are right here. Some of the herbs that come from other countries are fumigated and whatever that process does to them is very questionable. We should get things that come more naturally to us.

Herbs work both with the spiritual as well as the physical part of us. In the old days, if a person had a particular sickness, medicine people didn't always give the same herb for the same sickness, even if it seemed to have the same symptoms. There might be other things causing the sickness. The healer would go out to make a prayer to that herb and to the spirits that were there to find out if that was the right thing for the sickness.

Something that a lot of people are going to have to get back to is actually experiencing and learning how an herb works. They have to learn that it won't work quickly like a chemical. People have to get used to herbs taking a little longer. We use herbal teas for a lot of our sicknesses and problems. In the winter, we get some colds or sinus infections, and we use yarrow teas and some of the other good things that are around us. But the "cure" might take a little longer.

The more love you put into cultivating the herbs, the better off you are. You get a better return from them. I think people are now starting to understand that these changes that are coming to Earth Mother, the destruction and cleansing, are because man has been out of harmony with the natural forces. But when you come back into harmony and start appreciating plants and using them in a good manner, they start serving you again. Each part of the universe is part of the whole; we're all part of the medicine circle.

Wabun

The earth is a wonderfully patient teacher. If you open up a little bit she is willing to teach you everything you need to learn, even if you come from New York City as I did. I was a writer and also a person looking for a spiritual teacher when I heard about the work Sun Bear was doing. I am certainly not native by background. I'm Welsh.

Well, the difficulty initially, I think, was just in trusting that my intuition had brought me to the place where I was supposed to be. But as soon as I started being with the earth it just felt natural. It made me feel complete. And when I started learning about herbs it felt really good. I never imagined I'd be learning about anything like that. Fortunately, I've always been a person who learned better by listening to and watching other people. And this was the way native people taught.

One thing I've learned is to never limit your definition of a medicine person. It's not just somebody who works with herbs. A medicine person is a sacred person. Perhaps their medicine, their work, doesn't have anything to do with herbs at all. Maybe they bring about healing in other ways, or maybe they are beyond the point of doing healings at all. Perhaps their work is strictly teaching and guiding.

Usually herbalists are considered to be medicine people of a certain degree. But in times past their work might encompass what today we would call the work of a doctor, a psychologist, a counselor, or teacher; they could fill all of those functions at one time.

There were many women among the native people who

71

Sun Bear and Wabun
Spokane, Washington

were healers, and their training would be pretty much the same as for men. If you had a vision that you were to become an herbalist or a medicine person, then your vision would tell you what herbs to start working with. You might study with an herbalist, learn what he knew, and combine that with your own perceptions.

Probably the only restrictions placed on women healers was the moon time, the menstrual time restrictions. Originally these were not based on fear but on understanding. Native women understood the power coming through them at that time, and they understood that it had to be channeled properly so that it would bring good and not harm to the people. I can only explain this from experience. Anthropological information is almost nonexistent.

If women just try to experience their own feelings during menstruation, they will feel that they are less focused than they are at other times. Then, if they can learn, or be trained to focus that unfocused energy, they can accomplish great beings. But there are very few women enough in tune with their own energy and power to do that or to be able to teach other women how to do that.

Many herbs, sometimes called the "female herbs," having to do with pregnancy or childbearing, would only be used by women, not men. As far as any secret native tricks for birth control, I've met some medicine people who claim to have that knowledge, but they say it would just be abused so they don't pass it on.

Sun Bear says the average medicine man has knowledge of 150 different herbs. But I don't consider that I know an herb until I've gathered it and used it on other people or myself. I think if you have a dozen herbs growing nearby that you know well, you can probably do about as much healing with those dozen herbs today as you could if you had a much wider knowledge of herbs. A lot of people who go into herbalism do it in the same kind of encyclopedic way that people in this society tend to go into other things. They read 30 books on the subject and get themselves all confused. I think it is more to the point, if you want to be an herbalist, to go out and be with the earth and let the herbs start to teach you about themselves.

To native people there were four earthly kingdoms. The first kingdom was that of the mineral people; they have the ability to exist without the help of any of the other kingdoms. The second kingdom was that of the plant people; they can exist with the help of the mineral kingdom. The third kingdom is that of the animals; it takes the other two for those of the animal kingdom to exist. And we in the human kingdom are the fourth order of creation, and the most dependent. We cannot exist without the help of our brothers and sisters in the other three kingdoms.

Although we were given the power to have vision and carry it to fulfillment, in all other ways we are weaker than those in the other three kingdoms. So when you go out to gather, you say, I have need of what you have to give me for my life to continue; I have need of this herb to help cure a sickness that someone has.

You explain to the herb why you're picking it and what you want it to do. You don't go in and pick it quickly. You give it time to hear what you have to say before the picking takes place. You assure the plant that you too, at some point, will give the physical form you have to the Earth Mother so that the life of the earth can continue and the circle remain unbroken. As it gives its life, so we give ourselves, our lives, our energies so that others may live.

The earth is a very patient teacher, and one of the lessons we have to learn from her is about patience. You have to go softly enough to learn the rules, so you don't offend people. You have to listen and wait.

Let things come to you as they are supposed to. Maybe that's the best lesson people will learn if they try to learn herbal healing from a native medicine person—slow down, be more respectful.

A tall, slender man with large dark eyes, *Nam Singh* explains that there "is no distinction between medicine and food to the Chinese. Food is medicine." Chinese medicine involves restoring the balance between yin and yang energies of the body, which can be done through the use of herbs.

Nam Singh began his herbal studies at the age of five at a Taoist Temple in Taiwan. Over the years, along with learning the art of T'ai Chi Ch'uan, meditation, breathing exercises, and priestly magical rites, Nam Singh has studied herbs both in the field and in the laboratory. Presently, he teaches in and serves as an administrator for several California healing centers.

Nam Singh
Sonoma, California

Nam Singh

In China, in the olden days, you paid the doctor only when you were well. But now Western influence has crept in so you have to pay him even if you get sick. Depending on the village, the Chinese doctor was set up by the villagers in such a way that he had in his house what he needed to live. As soon as people started getting sick, however, the villagers would stop supplying him with his daily rice and other necessities.

In those days, whatever your trade was, you became a master of it. If you were brought up in a tradition of medicine, you would learn it from your father and from other doctors, but you would hardly ever go to a school. The trade was just passed down through the generations.

My own family comes from a long tradition of medicine. My great-grandfather was a doctor, an undertaker in the Philippines who went to mainland China to study Chinese medicine. Then my grandfather followed in his footsteps as a doctor. He wanted to go to mainland China to join his father. But before he could even get out of the Philippines, my great-grandfather passed away, which curtailed my grandfather's plans for getting to mainland China. So he relocated in Taiwan. But he always kept the desire to get to mainland China. Today, I have that same desire.

When I was five years old, I moved from the United

States to Taiwan to live with my grandparents. When I got there I entered into the Dragon Temple, which was a traditional school of Taoist studies. They accepted me only on my grandfather's merits as a doctor, so before I enrolled he gave me a crash course on mannerisms—what to do and not do. My first year was a "trial" year. Everything I did was closely watched all the time. My biggest job was sweeping the courtyard, which just seemed to me like miles because I was so small. I was a pretty calm child, so, fortunately, I took to the program quite easily.

Our schedule was very rigid. We would get up at 3 a.m. to sit in meditation and then do exercises and make offerings. At 5 a.m., we'd do Tai Chi. That was followed by breakfast, which was followed by academics—reading, writing, arithmetic, and so forth. Then, when I was about 12 years old, I started my actual training in herbal medicine.

This training was also very rigorous. Primarily, it was practical application and memorization. That's the key to education in China—memorization. But it's done in a very natural way. For example, we would be out in the fields and our teacher would show us an herb and tell us how it could be used. Then he would show us how it worked by applying it to one of us. We learned the structures of plants, how they grow, what families they are in and how to gather and prepare the herbs.

As I grew older, the training became even more intense, and I was taught in a Chinese-style laboratory (more like a large kitchen). We never learned about any herb without it being right in front of us.

The school was unique. The only other place in Taiwan where I could have acquired that information would have been in a traditional medicine school. Our teachers were very good at what they taught. They also struck such a spark for individuality! I studied there for eight years, left for awhile, and then went back for another four years.

When I was living in Taiwan and going to the Taoist school, I would sometimes go home and stay with my grandparents. My grandfather lived out in the country. He had built up a name for himself, so the people who lived in the small towns would come to him. When he was busy treating patients, he would ask me to help him by giving tea to the people who were waiting, or, sometimes, he would ask me to change the sheets. That became my job. Then, when I got to be a teenager, he started actually teaching me about acupuncture, the meridians, and the theory behind Chinese medicine.

The way you could tell a good doctor was by how many patients he had. The more patients he had, the better. My grandfather had to be very aware of all his patients. He had to know all about herbs and acupuncture and also about each of his patient's social and mental characteristics.

Actually, the Chinese doctor's title should be "holistic practitioner"—the Western doctor better deserves the title of doctor. The Chinese doctor looks at the body holistically through all the ways, from the spirit to the marrow. He sees everything. The Western doctor is more intellectual and works with the symptoms. So this is a distinction.

In mainland China today, medicine is very, very good. They use the good of both worlds. They are using scientific as well as traditional medicine, and they say this creates an entirely different type of health care. There is a lot to be said for scientific medicine. We have crossed many bridges. Through scientific procedures, we can process the herbs—make them into extracts—so the body can assimilate them more quickly. Mao insisted that the Chinese who study Western practices also study traditional medicine.

Of course, the structure of Chinese medicine is related more to the people than ours is. Their income is lower, but everyone is taken care of. If you need an operation, you get an operation. If you need medicine, you get it. The fact that you can get an operation in China for under $100 is really hard for us to comprehend. But that's the way it is. You see, if you allow society to become full of sick people, you're not very strong as a nation. And China wants to be very strong.

An important difference between herbs and chemical medicine is that many chemicals weaken the body and make the body dependent on them. Herbs do just the opposite. Herbal medicine strengthens the body, although it may take longer to have an effect. If you go to a Chinese apothecary shop, the herbalist is not just someone who fills the prescription; he also must have knowledge of Chinese medicine. He can take your pulse and determine whether you are weak or strong. He prescribes the herbs you need. But you must come back so he can take your pulse again and see if they have worked. The people always have a choice between Western and Chinese medicine in China today. Sometimes they take the scientific approach by making herbal medicine into pills so they are easier to take.

Because there is no real distinction between medicine and food, food is medicine. In everyday preparations the Chinese use many things, like lotus root or ginko nuts. Some of them are vegetables, some are herbs, but they are combined with food, so there is no difference. They are one and the same. Even if you are not sick, taking herbs every day helps to prevent sickness. This is what is really important, their attitude on health is preventive.

The proper way for Americans to use Chinese medicine is, first, to find a competent herbalist—a Chinese herbalist or someone who is knowlegeable in Chinese medicine. He or she can advise you efficiently on how to prepare and use the medicine. Usually you have to shop around to find an efficient herbalist. If you are a foreigner in China, this may not be easy. You may have to prove yourself. That's something in the Chinese blood. But if you get closer, through your consistency and patience, they will accept you more and more.

In this country, because Chinese medicine isn't generally accepted, practitioners find interesting ways of working. They usually are not classified as doctors in this country. At most herbal stores you are not buying medicine. That's good. It is a tea. It is classified as a tea, a food product. In fact, that's exactly what it is. The older Chinese doctors are very cautious because of bad experiences in the past and also because they inherently tend to be very cautious people. They look to see what your intention is, not so much by superficial appearance but more by the root of what you want, the real essence of what you want. Some of this has to do with practical problems of the American Medical Association not accepting acupuncture and herbal medicine, but it goes much further than that. This is just the way the people are. They are very tight, family-oriented, strong villager-type people. If you make good friends with a Chinese person he'll be your friend for life, but if you disappoint them it's a very distressing situation.

Although the Chinese have been using their form of medicine for more than 2,000 years, when you get the Chinese and Western herbalists together, there is hardly any difference. Herbs provide a universal language—they are plants, and dealing with plants is the same anywhere. Everywhere you go, there are herbs. Of course, they vary in size and appearance and so on, but they are just about the same everywhere. An example is plantain; you can find it on almost every continent—even in Alaska. The only differences are in the rituals and ways of going about the practice of herbalism.

He welcomes you with a smile that emanates warmly from his eyes, and reverently bows in acknowledgment of the introduction. Behind this ancient formality lies the soul of a happy child, eager to set aside protocol and share his knowledge and joy. *Dr. Vasant Lad* is an Ayurvedic physician from India. His conversation is enthusiastic and colored with innocent humor. He speaks the language of Ayurveda, which he calls "the science of life."

When Lad came to America in 1979, he brought with him a wealth of practical experience and understanding gained during the time he served as medical director of the Ayurvedic Hospital in Poona, India, and during 15 years of experience as a teacher of clinical medicine at the Poona College of Ayurvedic Medicine. Today, Lad is director of the Ayurvedic program at Santa Fe's Institute of Traditional Medicine.

Vasant Lad

People who first hear of Ayurvedic medicine may think of it as merely another sort of herbal science. This is not true. Herbal treatments are the most commonly used of all the Ayurvedic medicines, but in talking about Ayurveda we are sharing together knowledge about a complete science of daily existence. We are talking about an indigenous, holistic, and comprehensive system of medicine.

Ayurveda is a Sanskrit word. *Ayur* means life or daily living and *veda* is the knowing or learning. Ayurveda has its roots and substance in the ancient Vedas. For more than 5,000 years, this healing system has been practiced daily in the lives of individuals in India. Because of its origins, it is a very spiritual science. It is much more than a science of herbs or even a medical science.

Ayurveda sprang from cognitions that occurred in the meditative minds of the ancient seers of truth, called *rishis*. From the hearts of those enlightened beings, this intricate and comprehensive science emerged from the Cosmic Consciousness. Much of the original herbal wisdom has been lost to the ages. This knowledge was never written down; it was preserved through the oral tradition that was passed directly from guru to disciple. If the guru found no one worthy to be his disciple, the knowledge was withheld. Then, when the guru died, the knowledge

Vasant Lad
Santa Fe, New Mexico

died with him. Other Ayurvedic knowledge has been locked in the ancient texts of the Vedas. This Vedic wisdom requires study, contemplation and sometimes the understanding and interpretation of a guru.

Because this science of life has been practiced continuously for more than five millenia, the wealth of accumulated knowledge that forms the basis of Ayurveda is unparalleled in other medical traditions. Although most of the texts are still in the original Sanskrit, Ayurveda gives explicit directions for the collection and use of literally thousands of herbs. There are so many ways that herbs help on all different levels of physical and psychosomatic treatments.

For example, the inhalation of certain herbs will help to open the body's chakras (energy centers) and will help to release emotions that have accumulated in the crown chakra, which is the brain chakra. The beauty of such therapy is that it can restore complete balance to the breathing. Inhalation of some kinds of perfume or incense can also calm the heart.

In India, to become an Ayurvedic physician, one must study many subjects very hard—Sanskrit, mathematics, Eastern philosophy, and physiology. Accredited colleges of Ayurveda are affiliated with the government, and it takes five years to earn a certificate. The university that supplies accreditation also supplies the Ayurvedic courses to these colleges.

Each Ayurvedic college also has a training center that is really a full-fledged hospital. People from the cities and provinces can come there and receive treatment for free. Sometimes, if the patients are able, they leave a small donation. The students who work at the hospitals learn both hospital methods and charitable understanding. Then, after finishing their degrees, the students must serve one year internships. Only after this internship does the student receive a certificate to practice as an Ayurvedic doctor.

A doctor may open his own clinic, or he may learn a specialty, such as herbs. After I graduated, I received a master's degree of Ayurvedic science. Then, for more than 15 years, I taught at the Ayurvedic Medical College in Poona. Also, I was house physician and chief medical officer at the Seth Tarachand Ramanath Ayurvedic Hospital. I saw so many patients there that finally I opened my own private clinic, with the help of my wife.

In 1979, I was invited to come to this country by my American friend and assistant, Lenny Blank, whom I met in India. Lenny called me from New York and asked if I would come. I could hardly believe my ears! The first time he spoke to me on the phone, he said "good evening" and I said "good morning." Although I had only a scanty acquaintance with English, I could not refuse such an opportunity to share Ayurvedic teachings.

People are so beautiful here. They are open, and they have so much knowledge to offer. India, too, has much to share. Because India is not a wealthy country, we have learned simple methods of healing that rely on the daily use of herbs and spices. Such medicinals are relevant now that America is looking for alternative health methods. Even allopathic doctors who study the basic principles of Ayurveda are able to use this healing system as a complement to their own medicines.

Such a treasure of science is stored in the Vedas that scientists everywhere must open their eyes without prejudice. If I say that my science is *the* science and that others are not valid, then I am closed. We all must open. It is always possible that another kind of healing system works equally well. Ayurveda teaches harmonizing of conflict and integration of medical practices.

When I was young, I thought I wanted to be an allopathic physician. Even though my guru had told me when I was just a boy that one day I would come to the West to share the ancient Ayurvedic science of health, I still felt that my vocation was the practice of allopathy. Then, one day my grandmother became very ill, and my uncle's friend, an allopathic doctor, was called in to help her. He treated her for about a month, but she just kept getting worse. She had complete renal failure, her blood pressure shot up, and her kidneys failed altogether. At that time, we had no such thing as kidney transplants or dialysis.

My father was not an Ayurvedic practitioner, but he was a strong believer in natural remedies. In a way, he was also a healer. If someone had a cough in the night, a bug bite, or asthma, he could treat them with the help of certain herbs. Anyway, he had a friend who was the dean of faculty at the Ayurvedic Medical College and he came to see my grandmother.

He just examined her pulse and prescribed a proper diet and a certain herb with a very beautiful healing action. In 15 days, my grandmother was completely well.

After that, my father asked me again, "What is allopathic medicine? Why do you like it so much?" I couldn't answer him. So, my father said, "Look, can't you see the difference between those two doctors?" He was very adamant. Then he told me he would get me admission into the Ayurvedic college. "Bring all your papers," he said. And so I applied and received admission.

In my college studies, I learned the science behind my grandmother's healing. In treating particular illnesses through Ayurveda, we don't say "Do this," or "Don't do that" in a general way. Each person is treated as an individual with a completely unique constitution. From a study of the five elements of Space, Air, Fire, Water, and Earth, we know that each person's constitution is determined by the ratio or combination of these elements.

All life processes can be categorized in terms of three bodily humors—*vata*, *pitta*, and *kapha*. In Western medicine, these might be called "wind," "bile," and "phlegm" or another Western translation might be "catabolic," "metabolic," and "anabolic." According to Ayurveda, the degree of harmony or imbalance among these three constitutional elements is responsible for a person's state of health. Thus, the status of the three humors is diagnosed before any therapeutic herbs or medicines are prescribed for an ailment.

Other diagnostic techniques also employ holistic knowledge of the body. For example, if the kidneys are bad, we know the second chakra is at fault. Treatment therefore focuses on healing the person's second chakra, to give him energy. The Ayurvedic physician *(vaidya)* may also suggest certain meditations, so that the individual will not store his feelings and emotions in that chakra. Once a patient becomes aware of the ways that his energy is blocking a certain chakra, then the *vaidya* can help him to focus that energy and just release it. If he does not release the block, then the same health problem will reoccur in a few years. Suppression of the symptom does not cure the illness. Rather, Ayurveda focuses on complete eradication of the basic cause of the disease.

Ayurvedic philosophy is based upon the interrelatedness of all things in the cosmos. We see disease as nothing more than the individual's imbalance with his external environment. The Ayurvedic treatment is the process of restoring harmony between man and nature. Because early man had to be highly intuitive about nature in order to survive, he was intimately aware of the effects of eating this or that plant. He did not know the science of today's Ayurvedic practice, but he knew that by chewing a certain leaf, root, or bark he could restore his healthful balance. He watched the animals and then tasted the plants himself.

Certain herbs may help in the healing process. The actions of some herbs, for example, will work upon the kidneys. Coriander is a common spice used in cooking both in India and America; however, the Vedas explain that coriander is also a powerful medicine. A tea of the coriander seeds will act as a urinary alkaline. In some cases, when one feels a burning sensation when passing urine, the cooling and diuretic properties of coriander can serve to alleviate the problem.

In Ayurvedic practice, we never give antibiotics, steroids, or chemical diuretics. Such diuretics will cause the patient to lose iron and become easily fatigued. Then his blood pressure may shoot up. By diagnosing the basic cause and treating it with natural remedies, we work to eradicate the illness completely.

In a certain way, Ayurvedic pharmacology is a science of evolved tastes. Various tastes can be classified according to how they affect the body and the mind. An example is provided by a fat person who diets and diets and never seems able to lose any weight. It may be that even the small amounts of food the person is eating are not right for his condition. Overweight people should eat foods having pungent and bitter tastes. These foods actually heat the system and act to balance the overweight person's inborn tendency to put on fat.

Licorice provides another example of taste-related healing properties. Licorice is sweet and slightly astringent to the taste. These attributes make it a natural expectorant. Not only does licorice clean the mouth, but it increases secretions to the entire gastrointestinal tract. Thus, licorice is very effective when used for peptic ulcers and gastritis.

If you chew on a stick of licorice, it will clean your mouth and even arrest tooth decay. It has a wonderful germicidal action. And then, of course, if you have a cold or cough, you can make a tea to help in expectoration. Sometimes licorice is even made into a medicated oil that can be used for severe colds, bronchitis, or tonsillitis. It can be very effective in alleviating repeated asthma attacks.

Before prescribing licorice, the Ayurvedic physician will feel the pulse and examine the entire body, studying it carefully to determine the correct form and proportion of the medication. Licorice can be administered in the form of tea with honey or taken with milk, or it can be made into a medicated ghee. Ghee is a very common product in India made from raw, unsalted butter.

One method of administration is to prepare a licorice decoction, which will allow every molecule of licorice to combine with every molecule of ghee. This licorice ghee can be taken internally—a medication that is beneficial for diabetes—or it may be applied externally on wounds.

Many times Ayurvedic physicians use their intuition, developed over years of meditation and study, to determine which herbs are right for a certain patient's ailment. When you receive strong intuition that an herb is good for such and such a thing, and then you check the texts and find that it has been used for centuries, then you begin to know the science on an intuitive level. You can use your intuition and you will find that it works.

Many herbalists in this country say to collect the plants in the morning. In India, we say to take the plant in the evening, when there is a lunar energy and the rays coming from the moon nourish the juices of the plant. At the time of high lunar energy, it is beneficial to sit near the plant and meditate on its energy.

Ayurveda is a holistic science, utilizing the healing properties of not only herbs and metals but also gems and colors as well as yogic practices. The American mind is so finely tuned to appreciate science that soon it will discover the profound depth of the many branches of Ayurvedic medicine. Already this is happening. There are even computerized translations of the ancient texts. The seeds of Ayurveda are beginning to sprout in the American soil. But Ayurveda is more than scientific knowledge. The Ayurvedic physician must work with love in his heart.

Then, and only then, will his treatments restore harmony.

Ayurveda is very ancient; however, its wisdom is also very powerful and scientific. At first its basic methodology may seem strange to the Western mind, but America is now becoming mature, and she is open and ready to learn these secrets that for so many centuries have been hidden deep within the womb that is India.

A lively woman with a straightforward manner, *Billy Joe Tatum* abandoned a career in classical music to become a doctor's wife. But when her children became ill, she began using medicinal plants to heal them. Using remedies taught to her by "Aunt Tenny," an elderly mountain woman, Tatum saw that the teas worked, and soon her incidents of success rivaled those of her husband.

She usually calls herself a "woodsie," an old Ozark term for a naturalist. From their Ozark mountain home, "Wildflower," the Tatums frequently entertain guests at elaborate herbal banquets. In addition, Billy Joe makes appearances on various radio and television programs, teaches, and still finds time to gather, dry, and package her own herbal teas for distribution to numerous stores.

Billy Joe Tatum

Learning about herbs is just like finding out about birds. Pick out a nest, figure out the way it's made, admire the craftsmanship, and then find out what kind of bird it is. Birds, in that way, are like people; you can't really know them until you "get into their nest." The same way, you can't really know a plant until you've worked with it and seen it grow from seed to picking.

Although today it's not unusual for me to meet my friends out in the field, 25 years ago I didn't want people to see me out there gathering herbs—with my kids tagging along behind me. I thought they would think I was strange, but I did it because I couldn't bear to see fields of sweet goldenrod (*Solidago odora*) and other herbs going to waste; I gave bags and bags of the tea away.

I also have to admit, I went to the fields to get control of myself; I did it to calm myself down. When you have several small children, you have to try to maintain a balance. I always felt that if I could just get the kids into the woods, I could relax a bit. My husband was the town doctor and, fortunately, we lived not far from the open fields, so it was an easy thing to do. The kids who weren't in school would dig around with me all day long in the fields.

When I first started out I looked for wildflowers. I was so unfamiliar with botanical books that I couldn't even

Billy Joe Tatum
Melbourne, Arkansas

figure out the identification keys. So I memorized my first book from cover to cover. It was called *Spring Flora of Missouri*, by Julian Steyermark, and it's still one of the finest books around for wildflowers for our area.

About the time I was getting interested in flowers, my husband discovered that his patients were using lots of home remedies, and he started jotting all these teas and formulas down on their charts. Before long, however, we found out that his patients' home remedies were the same as my wildflowers. So together we began collecting, and soon had literally thousands of cards on the remedies which almost always include herbs.

One of my first remembrances of learning remedies from a patient is from the day I trekked into Harold's office with all four kids in tow. I was just absolutely worn to a frazzle by having a houseful of kids with colds and runny noses. Most of the time, he would be so tired when he came home from the office that I just couldn't see bothering him with another runny nose. But that day, feeling so frazzled, I decided I would try a trick of doctor's wifery; I would just go and sit in the front office and wait for an appointment. And that was the day I happened to meet up with Aunt Tenny. This little old lady started talking to me and invited me to her house and made me a wonderful cup of soothing tea. Before long, she had me convinced that I should drink calming teas, give the children catnip for sleeplessness and use dittany tea to lower temperatures. I hated giving the kids aspirin. You know a small youngster doesn't need to be taking aspirin every week, and yet, sometimes we're inclined to just pop one in his mouth because a kid will chew it up, swallow it down, and maybe, for a while, maybe feel a bit better. But Aunt Tenny showed me the plant in her garden that she called fever plant. Right away I started experimenting, and I soon discovered that three or four cups of dittany tea would reduce fever as quickly as ten grains of aspirin.

It's funny, but it took me several years before I could identify the plant in the field because I could never find it when it was flowering. In botany, you cannot identify a plant accurately without its flower, so I just laughed when I finally discovered its secret. It turns out dittany flowers in the fall, and the whole time I had been looking for it in the spring and summer. When my kids were little they drank dittany tea with sugar, honey, and milk, but Aunt Tenny made me realize that it was very important to put children's tea in a beautiful, little china cup with a pretty picture on it. She knew all the secrets.

Although there aren't too many people in the Ozarks today like Aunt Tenny, who still grow their own herb gardens, it used to be a common practice. For years I went around collecting plants for my own garden from the gardens of old homes around here. Almost every house in the area here has catnip out around the chimney. Horehound grew in the garden and pennyroyal grew all over the place. Rue is another plant they used a lot. Anise escaped from somebody's herb garden, and now grows wild on the East Coast.

People around here, even today, just use these things naturally. Once I approached this old-timer and asked him if he had an herbal remedy for coughing. He just laughed and said we don't use herbal remedies. But there he was, sitting in the sun and teaching his grandson how to smoke mullein, which is good for congestion. Pretty soon his wife came out of the house and said, "How about a little blackberry root tea for this boy. He's got a summer complaint."

Most rural people during the Depression used herbs at one time or another, and many of them still do. Today, when I find people smoking mullein for upper respiratory problems, I tell them not to inhale it, just smell it. If you sniff it, mullein cuts the phlegm just as effectively and still helps to reduce the inflamed and swollen membranes. For upset stomachs people commonly drink peppermint tea or else horsemint or ginger and think nothing about it. They don't go through the thought process anymore than you or I would think about picking up one foot and putting it in front of the other to take another step. It's just what they grew up with.

I've discovered all these things mainly by talking with people. Because I came here as a doctor's wife, I was immediately accepted and placed kind of on a pedestal. People have been willing to share their knowledge with me. But, of course, to really get to know them takes more than just being a doctor's wife. Mountain people will treat you as an equal only if you really are equal. Honesty is what they look for.

Today my husband uses a few herbs in his practice, although he's still quite concerned that some people may end up using herbs on their own for the wrong ailments. He quite literally uses gallons of aloe vera. It's especially helpful with his poison ivy patients. He'll occasionally use other herbs, too, whatever seems to be the right way to go. Once a friend of ours braved a blizzard to ask Harold what he would prescribe for his daughter's mastitis, which is an inflammation of the breasts. Our daughter had gotten over it, so my husband advised a comfrey poultice which he knew had worked beautifully. Harold wrote out the directions and that's what relieved her. He practices conventional medicine, more or less, but he's more inclined to suggest horsemint tea than Alka Seltzer. Of course, I won't diagnose anything; I'm a practitioner like any other housewife. Instead of Unguentine, I use pennyroyal. My methods are just different. I'd have to say, though, that three of my five children today would probably turn to my husband before me and my herbs if they wanted to get their warts burned off.

On the whole, doctors are starting to realize the need for learning more about medicinal plants. In fact, it seems as if hardly any time goes by at all, when some doctor isn't calling me up to find out about the effects of such and such a plant. An optician called me just the other day to find out why this seven-year-old child's pupils were dilated. After a few questions, I knew what it was. The kid had helped clear the garden plot and had seen these little berries and eaten them. I described the plant, which was deadly nightshade, and later on he sent a seed just to verify it.

So here I am with one year of botany in college and a little in high school, but I've learned quite a bit about plants by reading and by going to the woods. Fortunately, I have a photographic memory where plants are concerned, so I can hold a candle to any Ph. D. botanist that comes along. Sometimes, when these doctors call me, my husband and I just laugh together about it. We have an exceptionally good relationship. He's never required any of the usual things of me, like laying out his clothes and all that. His only requirement is that all of us and the people in his office be happy and content.

Our home is called Wildflower; it's a great big A-frame, four stories high that looks out over 50 miles of Ozarks. Here my children help me gather and distribute herb teas. Sometimes, just for fun, we'll have these big dinner parties where we'll invite the governor and have things like wild turkey and rattlesnake canapés, along with mushrooms, wild strawberry tarts, mulberries, candied violets, watercress soup, dandelion wine, and dittany dip. I make most of my own crackers and breads, and I bake acorn bread in a solar oven. You can cook each edible plant in about 70 or 80 different ways, but there's simply no end to the herb combinations.

When my daughter had her baby, she had a wonderful home delivery and we did all the things we knew about. She drank raspberry tea to help with the passing of the placenta, and then later we used comfrey and other herbs for muscle soreness. I guess to some it might seem strange when a family shares these things the way we do, but remember, there are just loads of people who are practitioners of chemical medicine and they never even know it. They'll say, "my doctor gave me this and it worked real well. Let me give you my decongestant or tranquillizer to try." We're all pretty good at passing around whatever medicine we're using. But at least, in our family, we get to hear about all types of medicine—we mix the modern with the traditional.

Countless folks have beaten a path to *A. L. (Tommie)* *Bass'* place in rural Leesburg, Alabama. Bass thrives on this attention and says, "It's a wonderful life. . . . I haven't made any money, but I've made a lot of friends all over the country."

A farmer who has lived in the area all his life, Bass became familiar with herbs by living close to the land. He tells people that the finest medicine grows right in their yards.

A jovial man, Bass has been harvesting and using herbs for more than 60 years. Several local doctors send their patients to Bass for specific herbs, which he is eager to supply.

A. L. (Tommie) Bass

I just took it up, you know, like a guy would take up using tobacco. It was just the more I got into it, the more I wanted to investigate it. One discovery brought on another. When I was about nine years old I was helping out. Then I was a bee hunter, a trapper, oppossum hunter, and an herb hunter.

The more I studied herbs, the more interested I got. You're so close to nature. It's one of the most interesting hobbies to my way of thinking that anyone could take up. I would advise any young person, if they want a hobby they never can catch up with, why, take up the study of herbs.

My family came out of east Tennessee back in about the early 1900s, I would imagine, because I was born in 1908 in what we call Jackson County, Alabama. We came in 1917, here to Leesburg, Alabama, and we've been here ever since. I've been one place and then another, but I always made Leesburg my home.

We were farmers, more truck farmers than cotton farmers, but we did raise some cotton and some corn. We cut timber on the side. My daddy was a fur buyer and he also bought some herbs, but only a few. He bought ginseng, goldenseal, and mayapple. As far as fooling with the medical herbs, he didn't do that. I didn't catch it from my

101

A. L. "Tommie" Bass
Leesburg, Alabama

daddy there. And, anyway, he didn't have good eyesight, so he couldn't find the herbs very well. The fact is, my daddy never grew cotton until 1918; he had to grow some to get a place to live. Back in those days you couldn't rent a house to save your life unless you raised cotton. Nowadays in this same county, they don't care whether you even plant cotton. It's soybeans and cattle now. My daddy was an herb dealer all his life, but we would have been listed, on one side of the house, I guess, as farmers.

It's a rough area, heavy country—Lookout Mountain, Shinbone Mountain, and Wisely Mountain, and several other mountains around here. It produces quite a few different kinds of roots and herbs. Of course we don't have the ginseng and goldenseal on this side of the mountain, but we have mayapple, and pinkroot, and boneset. We have queen of the meadow and many, many other herbs that grow around here on the sunny, southern side of the field. We also have wild hydrangea—or the Indian name for it is silvanbark—and many other common herbs like hyssop and so on. But we don't have the ginseng, that's over on the northern side of the mountains.

I didn't know I had been fooling with these herbs as long as I have until a year or two ago. Why, a lady came by; she told me that I saved her daddy's life 50 years ago. I never thought about it—being 74 now—but I never thought about me saving somebody's life. I couldn't think about it.

But the lady came on and said, "Bass, don't you know me?" She called me Tommie.

I said, "No, ma'am, I don't."

And she said, "Well, you're just a big old liar," and commenced to laugh.

She said I lived just hollering distance to her once. "Don't you remember my daddy working on the railroad, getting paid about two dollars a day? I mean he worked from daylight to dark."

I says, "I remember where you lived and all like that but I don't remember saving his life."

"Well," she said, "you did. He took sick. We didn't have no money. You went in the woods and got some kind of herbs. Now, your mother might've made the tea. You got the herbs, whatever it was, and in two weeks daddy was back on the railroad section. He said to the day he died, you saved his life."

Now, I don't remember that. If I did, I'm thankful to God I did. But anyway, that was more than 50 years ago.

I've been fooling with the herbs, not for the money, you know, when folks come here. It's just wonderful to be able to do what little I have done. Having people of all colors come here. Many people say there are just as many black people as whites. I'm glad to answer any question that I know I can answer truthfully. But I don't answer if I don't know.

Schoolteachers come here. Eight pupils came here. There were three black girls and the rest of them were white. I don't see why schools don't teach something about herbs. It would be interesting. It just tickles them pink to talk about the plants. They were surprised about the medicine that's just growing out in the yard. Folks think you've got to go over in the mountains or out in the woods, you know, but we've got some of the finest medicine just out in the yard. Even the dandelion is one of the finest medicines we can get. And it's safe, no harm in it or anything. But anyway, these girls were just thrilled, you know. Of course, the teacher, she knew me ever since she was a child. Her father was a good friend of mine.

All over the country I have people come in here. I had one man and a woman said they traveled a thousand miles—they didn't do that all in one day—just to try to find somebody to tell them about herbs. They found people who knew all right, but when they found out they didn't want to buy anything, they clammed up just like terrapins, pulled their heads in their shells and wouldn't say nothing.

So they came in here. The lady had her notebook, you know, and the man looked at his wristwatch and said, "What do you get for talking to people about herbs?"

I said, "Brother, I don't get anything. I make my living in other ways. I don't make it with these herbs." "Well," he said, "we've been finding the people but they wouldn't talk."

I said to the lady, "Just have a seat." And we started in. She took her notebook, and the first thing she wanted to know is what boneset is used for. So I told her. I said it's used for many different things but more for coughs and colds and chills and fever. She put that down and then she wanted to know what rabbit tobacco and mayapple were used for. The fella was still looking at his wristwatch. I guess we talked 30 minutes or so.

Then he said, "Are you sure you don't charge?"

I said, "No, sir."

After a while, I said, "Now folks, I'm going to give you some advice and I don't charge for it. The best thing you can do now—and I'm telling you the truth—if you want to get the thing straightened out with educated people you go down to the bookstore, wherever you live"—they lived somewhere close to Montgomery—"you go to the bookstore and call for *Back to Eden,* or Culpeper [*Culpeper's Complete Herbal,* by Nicholas Culpeper]. They'll tell you just exactly what to do."

Gosh, when they found out, they went away real happy. Well, I never thought about them coming back, but the next Sunday, the same man and woman with two men and two more women came back. The other four were young people. They stayed an hour and a half or two hours and said, "We sure have enjoyed ourselves." Then I think one of them had a camera, and they took pictures of this little shack here and of me, too.

I told them, "Well, you hang the picture out in your 'tater patch and you won't have any potato bugs on your potatoes."

They said, "We're gonna keep this. Can we come back?"

I said, "Anytime. My door's open."

They haven't come back so far. But anyway, you have people like that. They come in from all over.

In my opinion—of course, I don't guess I'll be around here—but in my opinion, we'll have plenty of doctors coming up, who'll use natural herbs. One doctor told me when he retired he was going to come and get me to show him about several different herbs. He wanted to make a nerve tonic to build up a person's system. He's actually a doctor but he's going to make his own natural medicine.

And so I told him, "If you want to learn, I'll tell you about it. You get some books and read up on it. By the way, the answer's right over the hill."

I never had any trouble with the doctors. They've never been agin' me or for me because I don't recommend anything. All I do is have the herbs and tell people where to get them. I've never been no competition to no doctors. In fact, I have had doctors recommend sassafras and yellow-root and other different herbs to their patients, and the people would contact me to get them. They've already been ordering things—native plants and seeds. They knew that I'd be more apt to give them a fair deal. You hardly ever see doctors that are interested in herbs, but I think they're waking up now. They're beginning to recognize ginseng. I notice where a few doctors, once in a while, say something about ginseng making you tick. Many younger doctors, in my opinion, are going to get interested in ginseng.

Sometimes, doing this, you were looked down on as a witch or a worried lunatic or something. But it's not that way anymore. People are actually thrilled about someone who can tell them about herbs. Some people wouldn't be interested, but most of them, when you get them out here where the things is a growin', they just light up. It's amazing to think that you're walking over a drugstore and don't know it.

The most popular herbs we have in this area would be mayapple, pinkroot, and queen of the meadow; and calamus, when you can find it—it's used a lot. We can't find calamus too plentiful, but we can find plenty of mayapple. And then pokeroot, it's another one. It's a medicine. Of course, we have to handle it with care, you know, but it's a good medicine. We've got samson snakeroot, and we've also got what's known as black snakeroot. Of course there are different kinds of black snakeroot, but this is a genuine black snakeroot. And we have the black cohosh in quite a few places.

I'll tell you something about using these herbs. You take a sedative and all it does is do away with the pain, maybe. But you see, a person, a human being, was made out of the dirt, and we've got to go "back to the dirt" to get something to nurse this body. If you want to fix a microphone or a tape recorder, you've got to get plastic or rubber or whatever it's made of. But for your body, to fix it, you've got to get something that's growing out there. When you take herb medicine, it helps relieve the cause and the pain, too. That's why it's so much safer to take herbs than these sedatives. Maybe they don't work as fast, but when they do, it does more good.

Most everybody has peach trees around their home or some friend of theirs has. Just about anyone could have a jar of peach tree leaves or have them in a paper bag or something, to keep the worms out. And then if they have a sick stomach, make a cup of peach tree leaf tea. They can drink it like iced tea if they want to. It will give relief and it's a medical plant.

It's not just folk medicine I'm talking about. I could recommend several things that medical people don't recognize which would be as good a medicine to my way of thinking. We're talking about actual medicine. Of course, herbs are not a cure-all, mind you—none of the roots or herbs is that. If they was, the folks that handled them wouldn't go to the graveyard—and we see them in the graveyard, you know.

But people are starting to listen. In the last five years, this herb business has skyrocketed. I have a friend—a big herb buyer—who has two 18-wheeler trucks. He goes all over North Carolina and West Virginia and Tennessee. He buys here. I pick herbs here for him. He's buying southern barkroot and giving 60 cents a pound for it. He told me that some of the big pharmaceutical companies told him— and he goes direct to them, like McKesson-Robbins and all those folks that make the medicine—that in the next ten years the weeds out there are going to be worth more than the crops growing in the field. He says people found out how the Indians had 170 different roots, herbs, barks, and seeds, things they used for medicine. Well, of course, the white man thought at first that they were heathen and didn't know what they were doing. Now, some of our famous doctors have found out that all of our good medicine is founded on what the Indians already knew about. They've got synthetic stuff and all but still, the real good medicine is in the earth, and everybody is coming to it.

It's a great thrill. It don't make you feel big; it makes you feel humble—an uneducated fellow like myself, never having been to school—to have these people come from colleges, these teachers, and be able to help them. Of course, they can help me a lot and they do. Like talking to ladies' aid societies—why, they get a thrill out of it.

The last one I talked with, they had a check in a sealed envelope and all the ladies had signed it. I just laid it back on the desk and said, "Ladies, I don't charge nothing. I just wanted to talk with you." I gave them a copy of *Back to*

Eden for their library and another herbal. Every once in a while one of them will call me and say we checked out so-and-so and want you to know about it. Well, I'm glad to do that kind of work.

It's a wonderful life. I wouldn't trade what I've done for anything. No money. I haven't made any money, but I've made a lot of friends all over the country.

Two black men came here. They were diabetics and wanted some blueberry root and leaves to make a tea. They found out it was real good for them, to help with their diabetes. It was one of the coldest days we had, and I had an awfully bad cold myself. The poor fellows were in such a bad shape, but I couldn't get anybody to dig the root. I told them what it was but they said they didn't know what it was, especially in the wintertime.

So I took off, got a big sackful, and prepared it, and made it into a tea. Then later, the fellows came back—they were really heavy, overweight—and they said, "Well, sir, do you know what we did in church yesterday? We had a special prayer for you and asked the Lord to just keep you on."

It just doesn't make any difference, you know, black or white. Why, that makes you feel really good, you know, because that comes from the heart. They got what they came after. But, still, it does you good to think they are thinking about you even after they're gone.

CHAPTER THREE

Learning

THE UNITED STATES stands apart from many of the world's nations by offering no certified instruction for herbal practitioners. While the classified section of a major newspaper or a health food journal may list various institutions of herbal study, these schools are invariably nonaccredited by the usual accrediting bodies.

The better schools focus on the nutritional aspects of herbs and provide ample warning that certificates in no way provide a license to practice medicine. Nonetheless, an underlying danger exists if students feel prepared to treat people after receiving only a general course in plant identification and the briefest overview of human physiology.

Students wishing a scientific basis for their herb interests have few alternatives. Either they can go to another country, such as England (where certified training for herbalists is provided by way of the Medicines Act of 1968) or they can try their luck at a pharmaceutical college.

The latter choice might seem desirable were it not for the fact that pharmacy schools are primarily dedicated to

111

the development and delivery of chemical medications. A branch discipline called pharmacognosy focuses more on the basic constituents of plants but provides little of the nutritional information that herbalists need.

Those who seek accreditation for modern schools of herbalism, however, often find resistance on all fronts. On the one hand, the medical profession tends to dismiss herbalism as antiquated, while on the other hand, the herbalists themselves may prefer to keep their learning informal.

These herbalists remind us that until recently plant knowledge was common knowledge, passed down from mother to daughter, father to son, and generation to generation. Plant education either in the home or in the tribal society was a continuous process, thereby instilling in anyone the inherent right to find his or her own plants, inspiration, and education.

The voices that follow indicate the kind of dedication and perseverance found in today's self-taught herbalists. *John Lust* describes the training handed down to him by members of his German family and community. "By the time I was born," says Lust, "my father and uncle had already spent 25 years developing natural living and healing concepts in this country . . . [that] had been thoroughly established in Germany."

Jeanne Rose admonishes her fellow herbalists to honor and acknowledge the value of academic training wherever it may be found and applied to herbs. And *Jeannine Parvati Baker*, in a more free-spirited way, encourages us to keep our sights open so that we may learn from a variety of teachers.

As much as anything, the herbalists represented in this book indicate that herbal education is available in America. We must, however, dig deep to discover it.

John Lust was born into a world of natural healing. His uncle, Dr. Benedict Lust (known as the father of naturopathy) came to America from Germany to tell of the work of Father Sebastian Kneipp, a physician-priest who combined herbs with water therapy.

For Lust, herbs were a way of life to be used daily, both internally and externally, along with other natural health measures. "To me, the use of herbs was normal and not unusual," says Lust, a composed gentleman who speaks sincerely and humbly. His family operated a health food store and two health sanitariums for which they grew their own herbs and raised some of their own food.

After years of apprenticing in the sanitariums and working side by side with his Uncle Ben, Lust decided to enter also the publishing and education fields. His *Herb Book* has become a popular and respected reference on herbs.

John Lust
Greenwich, Connecticut

John Lust

Standard medical education just didn't suit me. I saw healing and health as primary, surely one of the most intimate and personal things in each one's life, but the standard medical program was just not right. My uncle fought it and I understood the fight. I was not militant like he was, but I was convinced that the only answer was education.

By the time I was born, my father and uncle had already spent 25 years developing natural living and healing concepts in this country, concepts that had evolved over centuries, and had been thoroughly established in Germany. My father was a baker who baked whole grain breads, a trade he learned in Germany. In those days all young boys had to serve apprenticeships, so my father became a baker. In this country, in New York, he, with my uncle, developed a very large health food bakery. And, of course, it was my uncle, Dr. Benedict Lust, who came to be known as the father of naturopathy.

When Benedict was very young, he emigrated here from Germany because, like so many others, he felt he would find more freedom and opportunity here. To support himself, he took a job as a busboy in a large hotel. But in those days the work was overwhelmingly hard and the hours long. Eventually, he became ill with consumption. The doctor told him he was going to die and suggested that he might as well go back to his homeland to be with his family.

He did go back to Germany, but instead of going home, he went to see a physician-priest by the name of Father Sebastian Kneipp, who used herbs in combination with a popular "water cure." Benedict demonstrated spectacular results. Not only did he completely heal himself, but he was so adept at acquiring information that Father Kneipp sort of took him under his wing. By the year's end, in 1895, Father Kneipp commissioned him to go back to America and tell the people about his method of healing.

At that point, my father was working in Florida as a baker, but when Uncle returned, he joined him in New York. Right away they started publishing natural health literature, and, together, they opened a store in 1896 which was actually America's first health food store. They called it the Kneipp Store. Of course they sold herbs because herbs were always an important part of Father Kneipp's methods. So Benedict and my father ran the business, and pretty soon Benedict also opened his health institute, where he began giving herb and water treatments.

In those days the various ethnic communities in America were very clearly defined. The immigrants who came to this country more or less segregated themselves into communities that were Irish, Polish, German, Jewish, Italian, and so on. Especially among the German people there were very close ties which didn't go much further than their own group.

All these German people usually knew about Father Kneipp in Germany and then, of course, they were also learning about Dr. Benedict Lust in America. The Kneipp Store was very well received because they found that certain nutritional habits were different in this country. The foods and the way they cooked them just weren't the same, so they came to the store when they wanted a more

natural type of nourishment. Often they bought the literature and then, pretty soon, they would get interested in
the herbs. Of course, the herbs were always a major part
of this process; they were used in a very practical way, day
by day. They cooked them as food, they used them for
medicine, and they made them into poultices and oint-
ments for external applications.

So this was what was going on for those 25 years before
I was born. I always say that my own book, *The Herb Book*,
contains two generations of information, my own and that
of my father and my uncle. I was born into this situation
where herbs and everything that went along with them
were an accepted way of life. In a sense, naturopathy was
already being taught—my father was producing the whole
grain and natural foods, unroasted peanut butter and all
those things. And then there was the store, a school, and a
publishing company. By that time two sanitariums were
underway, one in Butler, New Jersey, and the other in
Tangerine, Florida. From this nucleus, my Uncle Benedict
provided true naturopathy to tens of thousands of natural-
health seekers. His school, the American School of
Naturopathy, granted degrees in this healing art. And the
organization flourished even while, as a rule, it met severe
opposition from various sectors of orthodox medicine.

By "true" naturopathy—and there are many variations
today—I mean a system that relies on simple herbal remedies which are used in conjunction with fasting, exercise,
fresh air, water, sunshine, and, of course, natural diet. It
took hold right along with homeopathy in the late
nineteenth century. Of course, naturopathy could not prevent the triumph of chemical medicines, but, nonetheless,
it continued to survive because it offered something that
so-called modern treatments lacked, that is, relative simplicity with treatments which worked in harmony with life
and weren't antagonistic to it.

To me, growing up in that German community, it just

seemed to be the normal way to live, whereas other people might think of it as strange. Actually, it wasn't the publishing so much or the store, as the sanitariums which attracted most of the outsiders.

We always grew our own backyard herbs, up in New Jersey in the summertime and down in Florida in the winter. We had all the natural herbs and fresh fruits available to us anytime we wanted. I grew up with the usual educational process except that our lifestyle was such that we didn't accept standard medical doctrines.

After I graduated from high school, I found it virtually impossible to find a university that offered the sort of framework I wanted. I had to tailor my education to my needs and, in a way, sacrifice some of what you might call "qualified" credentials. I did this knowingly in exchange for what I knew would be most essential for my life's work. I sensed that someday I would have to carry the torch of our family's work, and I wanted to be qualified.

I studied independently. Fortunately, I was able to attend the American School of Naturopathy, and then I interned at the two sanitariums. Always I kept extensive records, which eventually went into *The Herb Book*. At the sanitariums, a medical doctor and a naturopath examined the patients, but when it came to the treatments and diets, Benedict or I would prescribe them. Each week, we would make up special formulas for all the patients and there were literally hundreds. After a while I became perfectly familiar with the herbs to be used and the methods of treatment. And that became my practical education.

Today there just aren't any sanitariums like my uncle's here in America. There are fat farms, beauty farms, and things like that. They have so-called health resorts but they're often a joke, even if they do cost $1,000 a day. It's a joke when they miss the basic idea. Just the same as a tree is part of nature, so is man. All living things are a part of nature, and that relationship is the key to why and how you can lead a healthy and productive life. The less you do to interfere with that harmonious relationship the better off you are.

I still go back to Germany, to Father Kneipp's, where Uncle learned and where he was cured. I like to go back there and stay for four to six weeks—whatever it takes. There's nothing that you can do quickly. When I'm there, they conduct their methods the same way we did at the Yungborn Sanitariums. Herbal medicines are given in the form of tea or extracts of the herbal juices. I keep records of these and note them in my cure booklets.

Benedict was a visionary. He could see clearly through all the things that were going on. Still, his life ended sadly. In 1943, his sanitarium in Florida burned to the ground. He tried to save others in the building, but he was severely injured from smoke inhalation. Against his will, they hospitalized him and dosed him with sulfa drugs. After that he was just terribly depressed and he suffered greatly from lung problems.

Two years later, when he was still tied up with legal ramifications from the fire, he came to the New Jersey sanitarium for a visit. By that time, he was 74 years old, and I guess he decided that he'd just had enough. He died that weekend, but they never could find any medical cause for his death.

After his passing, I had to decide whether or not to keep the sanitariums going or to do my educational work. He left a tremendous empire and I was his only heir to carry it on. To me, the educational approach seemed to be the only effective way to reach large numbers of people, and, fortunately, I seem to have a gift for it. Some have ventured to describe me as America's foremost teacher of natural living, but be that as it may, I am grateful for the wisdom of my youthful decision.

The books I have written and the millions of books that I've had circulated have helped pave the way for what the younger generation is now picking up on. Today there is hope for herbalism and natural healing. And, of course, help has come from many quarters. The debt to plants as the original sources of modern medicines is today more readily acknowledged by the scientific community than ever before: things like quinine from cinchona bark, morphine from the opium poppy, digitalis from foxglove, the tranquilizer reserpine from rauwolfia, ephedrine from mahaung, as well as many others. As the excesses of our so-called modern civilization and its inherent waste become increasingly apparent, we can now look back and find that there's something worth saving in those old customs, with their whole grain breads and their herb treatments. Today, there's hope that herbalism as practiced for thousands of years can coexist successfully with Western-style medicine.

I knew it had to come. In many ways, my *Herb Book* led to modern investigations. Surely, up until now a large segment may have been holding back but it's such a practical thing. The study of herbs provides you with a survival skill. People are starting to develop the skills of self-reliance, and once again herbs are becoming a positive aspect of that development. Simplicity and self-reliance are the answers to many of our problems.

A striking woman with long, shiny black hair, *Jeanne Rose* is constantly on the go. Almost each minute of her day is planned in advance, a needed skill for her active life as author, herbalist, and businesswoman.

Like many herbalists, a serious breakdown of her own health caused Rose to become involved with plants. While recuperating from a paralyzing auto accident, she eventually restored her health through a combination of herbs, exercise, nutrition, vitamins, and positive thinking.

To study herbs, Rose espouses a combination of academic training mixed with instinct. She has a degree in zoology and has done postgraduate research in intertidal ecology, fungicides, pesticides, and honey bees.

Jeanne Rose
San Francisco, California

Jeanne Rose

The thing about herbalism is that when I started working as an herbalist over ten years ago, there was hardly anyone else in the field. Hardly anyone was talking about it, writing about it, or giving classes. See that little pointy house over there? That's where I wrote my first book. That's where I did some of my earliest herbal research. I felt like some sort of medieval witch—pointed towers, pointed hat. If you messed with herbs in those days, ten years or so ago, you had to be a witch or a cook, right?

I want to get our herbal life out of the underground and onto the above ground with a little more academic background and training. There is not a thing wrong with having book knowledge. There are a lot of my compatriots who just despise anything that comes out of a book, because it doesn't come from the heart and soul—the great stream of consciousness where all the God-given knowledge is to be found—but that's a wrong attitude.

Basically, we all learn in the same ways; we learn from other people, through our own experiences, and through the written-down knowledge from centuries ago. But it doesn't just come out of the ether to our brains and through our mouths. I want people to feel that it's okay to learn from other people through books as well as through verbal knowledge and wisdom.

Many of the herb books are old-fashioned, and they don't contain bibliographies. There's nobody in the world who gets complete and total knowledge from himself. What a bibliography is, is a map from zero knowledge to more complete knowledge. It's just a map of the way-stations from where you have started to where you are now. If I pick up an herbal and there's no bibliography, instantly that's a zero book because none of us started from scratch like that.

You see, whenever you research anything, you'll find things which confuse you or raise questions. It's like the center of a big spider web. There you sit, following all these strings out to their ends. Then you bring it all to-gether and, lo and behold, the whole beautiful puzzle fits.

As far as books are concerned, I started my herbal studies in book reading many years ago in college. Later I had a serious automobile accident. At the time, I'd been making clothes for rock-and-roll stars. We used to stage fashion shows with live music and dance. Groups like "Country Joe and the Fish" played, and then we would have our models jump up and down on little pedestals and do the rock-and-roll dances.

Anyway, I had gone down to Big Sur to the Pebble Beach Country Club, where I was doing a fashion show. I had all my rock-and-roll jackets and clothes packed in the car when I had the accident. I was damaged and my car was destroyed. The accident, I guess, was more important than the rock-and-roll trips because the accident gave me the time to sit and bring things together in my mind. I was paralyzed, mostly on the upper right side of my body. My arm was dead weight—like a stone—and my shoulder was just about immovable.

My first book, *Herbs and Things*, is the result. It's the accumulation of my notes for 20 years. I have files on this and that—you name it. When I was a Girl Scout I used to take notes on how the American Indians used plants for healings—which I thought then was totally nonsense. But since then I've really come around—180 degrees. But I had these very extensive files from the time I was five years old. I'm an academic enthusiast. So there I was paralyzed with nothing better to do. I had one little 25-cent herb book which I used to start putting potpourris together. Everytime I saw a strange term like balm of Gilead I thought, "Wow," because I had read the Bible from front to back one summer and I knew balm of Gilead. It just rang bells. So I started researching—and whenever you read anything you find out things that are confusing or put question marks in your mind. (It's like that spider web with all those strings.) So if you see the words balm of Gilead then you go back to the Bible, and all of a sudden you see myrrh and aloe and wonder what they are. Then you have to take myrrh and aloe and you have to get to those botanical books to see what they are, what kinds of plants they are. Are they shrubs, elephants, trees, what are they?

But you have to remember that by the time of my accident, I had also accumulated quite a bit of academic training. I had a degree in zoology from San Jose State College and had worked on a master's in intertidal ecology from the University of Miami Marine Laboratory. (In addition, I've done research on pesticides, fungicides, and honey bees, and studied plants like cucurbits and grapes.) Well, after a while, I got to the point where I realized that with my academic knowledge, plus that intrinsic knowledge that I had been collecting all the time, I knew more than was in the herb books that I was reading. I looked at these herb books, and it seemed perfectly obvious to me that they had been written, even copied, from the reading of other books. Some of the authors hadn't the vaguest idea of how to put the formulas they mentioned together. So I had these old fifteenth- and eighteenth-century herbals, and I'd take a recipe out of one and try to make it. (Of course, you have to learn all that old English, all those funny old words.) You just have to stretch the limits of your imagination and take in all the bits and pieces of information.

So I started making recipes. Then I'd write notes on it, on how to adapt the recipe from 500 years ago to bring it up to date with the tools and equipment and knowledge that I had now. I started applying some of those things to myself—recipes that said, "This will cure paralysis." And, you know, I did cure my paralysis. It took me about six months. It's really interesting.

Of course, there is no one real cure. I had a lot of work to do. It's a combination of exercise, nutrition, vitamins, positive thinking, plenty of laughter, and the herbal remedies. A big combination. There are no magic formulas anywhere.

People sometimes ask me what the doctors were doing while I was curing myself. I guess all I can say is that they were being doctors. I certainly don't dislike doctors. In fact, I often use doctors for their diagnostic tools and techniques. I mean, look, a doctor studies for around 12 years—more than any herbalist I know. Doctors learn from the thousands of patients they treat. And today, I know lots of doctors who are sort of on my side. I can pick up the phone and ask them, "How would you handle this? What would you do?" And there are even a couple of doctors who call me up and ask for help. Usually, they're the ones with patients who don't want to take their medicines. So I'll try to find a solid alternative route for them.

A network is beginning between doctors and herbalists but it's a cautious one. Herbal medicine, of course, is not taught per se. It seems that acupuncture has become a major category, and herbs have been relegated to a subcategory. But I have to admit I myself don't have much respect for many people who call themselves herbalists.

There are some in my profession who are better speakers than others. They may seem to be more dynamic and interesting, but that doesn't mean they're more knowledgeable. A couple of people—and I include myself here—whenever we teach we never put any initials after our names. That's because lots of those initials don't mean anything in the United States. Some time ago I got a phone call from somebody who wanted to know if I would pay him $500 for a one-week study. Then, at the end of the week, he would give me a degree of some sort or another. Can you tell me how anybody can learn a body of knowledge about the human being, the anatomy and physiology of natural things—herbal and botanical—in a week? Does that kind of degree have any sort of validity whatsoever? Of course not.

And then you have your correspondence courses. I've received material from lots of correspondence courses and they seem so out of date. They cost hundreds of dollars and they're sometimes just that school's brand of religious enthusiasm. I believe in the gods, in plants and snails and the other creatures, but I don't want anybody to tell me that I can't study herbal medicine unless I believe in their particular view of God.

Fortunately, things are changing. More and more, we're becoming a knowledgeable society. So read books, study, and question. Don't hesitate to go to a university bookstore and buy a really decent human physiology and human anatomy text. Get some herb books with bibliographies. I have about 500 herb books. But also, we have to know our own backyard. It's always important to remember that herbs are only one part of a natural cure. Exercise, diet, fresh water, and good air are all vital. It's always the right combination of treatments that works the best.

Jeannine Parvati Baker calls herself a "plant psychologist." A soft-spoken woman with a graceful manner, Parvati Baker has learned from a variety of teachers, but adds that she has a feminine approach to plants acquired from her friendship with other women herbalists.

"Plants were my greatest allies keeping me healthy in body and spirit," says Parvati Baker about her experiences with growing herbs during several pregnancies. Consequently, Parvati Baker's children enjoy a close association with plants through the use of daily herb teas and romping in their mother's herb garden. As a practicing midwife, Parvati Baker's approach to healing involves both spiritual and physical principles.

Jeannine Parvati Baker

Along the way, I've met teachers; but, quite honestly, even they wouldn't call themselves teachers. I haven't really sat in people's classes and learned about herbs. My learning has always been by experience. Nan Koehler and Rosemary Gladstar have been instrumental, but if you'd ask them, they would say they never really instructed me. What I learned from them mainly was the reverence they have for plants—that kind of "rubbed off" on me. It was a deeply feminine approach to the world of plants. Most of my relationship with plants has been directly through the plants themselves and not through formal teaching.

I guess you might say that I approach the spirit in plants in a very green way. I'm not too sophisticated about the process. I acknowledge that I have, inside of me, a seedling called spirit, and I'm constantly amazed at how much that spirit needs to grow. I initially began approaching the spirit in plants by contacting my own spirit (which was nonverbal at that time), and later I found a real value of talking to plants. I'm sure you've heard about this from other people who love plants too. I'd talk to them about what to do for this or that process. But it took me a long time to be able to weed and prune, to discover what was really valuable.

On one level, I have this idea that everything I present is

Jeannine Parvati Baker
Felton, Georgia

nonfactual, a myth. And I don't mean that it's not true, it's just that when I talk about this fact and that fact, I'm really talking about my *experience* with those facts. And so I have this idea, this myth, that plants change just as the human consciousness changes. They reveal to us their purposes as we're able to handle the information. For example, an herbal that was written in the fifteenth century was really valid for that time, but I'm not so sure the properties still hold. I'm not speaking of just an evolution myth. It's more an involution myth, meaning that human beings are turning more inside to their own ways. We create realities through our desires, and then we project those desires out to what we call the material world and plants. For me the spiritual is the physical, and it's the trick of our particular romance language that we've divided them up in different realms. Although the physical teaches us again and again that form changes, the spiritual is an aspect of our being that always remains the same.

As far as this relates to herbs, it seems obvious that herbs and their functions are changing consciousness. No longer are we relying so much on traditional medical doctors and drugs to cure us. We are more often asking the sickness itself to reveal the cure. In this way, herbs become our allies, working with us.

Sometimes you wonder how it all got started that when you're sick you go to someone else. In ancient times people would go into the temples. Disease, of course, means literally that you're out of harmony with yourself. And herbs signify a way to restore that harmony.

A lot of my book *Hygieia* was written not so much to emphasize taking herbs to get rid of or overcome illness as much as to understand the whole point of illness. Hygieia was the Greek goddess of healing. Her mother was Epione and her father, Asclepius. It was Asclepius who has become known as the first empiricist or true medicine man in our Greek tradition. And it is his story of noticing an ailing snake being treated by another snake which is represented on the staff of Caduceus, the contemporary symbol of the medical profession. According to the story, after the one snake dies the other snake does this amazing thing; that is, he finds an herb and places it on his dead friend. And, lo and behold, the dead snake is revived. An herb to raise the dead! Asclepius then used the herb to bring a dead man back to life and for this he was killed—but before all this he had fathered three healing sisters: Hygieia, Iaso, and Panacea.

Although not much is known about Hygieia, I've entitled my book after her in an effort to change the way we look at healing. She is, in essence, the goddess within each of us who knows the grace of being healthy. I use her myth to help people see the importance of using their inherent abilities to get information directly from the plants.

We're all so wanting to have that expert, to have someone outside ourselves tell us about health. But when you come right down to it, there's really no better expert than "ourselves." We're the only ones who have lived in our own bodies. I don't do herb "walks" anymore. I don't say this herb is good for this particular ailment or that particular disease.

Along with my herb work, I've been a senior midwife for the past few years. I started out by teaching natural childbirth classes, where I witnessed lots of births with other doctors and midwives. When you're learning, it's important to talk to people with very different approaches and then to learn from your experience. For example, I never recommend herbs unless I've tried them first myself.

When my twins were born, I had some complications. That time I went to a hospital, but I took with me some shepherd's purse and bayberry bark tea. All I asked for was a pot of hot water for the herbs to help stop the hemorrhaging—which happened almost immediately. After that, I asked to leave the hospital, but the doctor didn't want to let me go. When I finally convinced him, he followed me all the way to the house. That way we got to see each other's worlds. I don't believe in limiting yourself to one way of doing it or just one doctor or teacher. When you see lots of different ways, that can shake you into realizing that you have to find your own way.

You have to be willing to walk through the door yourself. I like this image of an African tribe in which there's this pregnant woman who starts into labor. The problem is that she's on one bank and there's a river that flows between her and the other side. She has this very narrow tree limb that has fallen between these two banks, and she's to walk it, and when she gets to the other side she will be birthing. But the midwife can't walk with her. There's only room for one to make that journey. What she can do is ride next to her in a canoe. She can be up there to support the woman in case she falls in the water. She can help guide her and say "Yes, you can take another step now." One can never make that journey for another. So that's my feeling about herbs too.

What I basically feel I'm here to do is to be a bridge or liaison between two worlds. I'd really love to see the bridge formed between science and magic. Actually, scientific technology comes from magic. It's time to acknowledge its ancestry, to take account of where it came from.

Too many times we tend to take herbs literally. I'm mainly concerned with the essence and metaphor. We tend to take herbs only because we desire them, not because we really need them. Herbs are very powerful agents, and they should be used knowingly and sparingly. Herbs are also food—and the same rule still applies. When our desires match our needs, the essence is revealed. Herbs as allies, as catalysts, can bring healing, union, to our desire, body, and spirit.

CHAPTER FOUR

Careers

IN ONE WAY of viewing it, the very first business of America was the business of herbs. How often we forget that when Columbus stumbled upon the New Continent, his goal was not to find another country but rather to find a shorter route to the Indies, the revered source of spices and herbal medications.

In America, it turned out, the herbs, and particularly ginseng, were ripe for both picking and shipping. By the mid-eighteenth century, many native herbs were relegated to a secondary status, as Boston, New York, and Philadelphia evolved into key centers for exporting "sang." Ever since, demand for American ginseng *(Panax quinquefolium)* has been on the upswing.

For more than two centuries, ginseng exports increased gradually until, by 1964, more than $2 million worth of ginseng was being exported yearly. Eight years later, in the aftermath of former President Richard Nixon's trip to China, this figure quadrupled to $8 million. And within another eight years, by 1980, ginseng exports were figured at $39 million and still growing.

But the ginseng story is just the tip of the herbal iceberg.

135

Sales of herb products of all kinds have escalated in recent years. Celestial Seasonings began in a Boulder, Colorado, barn in 1971, when its original founders began gathering herbs for teas from the nearby mountains.

Since then, Celestial has expanded into a multimillion dollar business that presently faces competition not only from the new wave of herb tea distributors but also from the traditional black tea specialists, such as Lipton and Bigelow, which now offer their own herb tea blends.

Despite the corporate rivalries, much of the herb business has retained its grassroots connections. In the shadow of the industry giants can be found a new breed of businessmen and women. For many people who embark on the herbal pathway, starting a career or an herb business are the alternatives they dream of. Yet few actually pursue their dream, fewer succeed, and fewer still survive in the way they want to. *Carolyn Hutchinson* and *Ellwood Carr* are among the fortunate; they have survived without compromising their principles.

Whether you're operating a shop (like Hutchinson), or packaging, teaching, and distributing (like Carr), you'll have to deal with many different people, pay bills, and keep schedules. The work itself is rarely complicated, but it has to be done on time and done right. You can't afford to mislabel a tea blend or give someone the wrong advice.

Despite the obvious risks and responsibilities, neither Hutchinson nor Carr would trade their careers for anything. Hutchinson confesses that she would make more money if she sold vitamins and other supplements, but she prefers to use her shop as a showcase to impress upon people the importance of getting proper foods and teas. Both admit that the money doesn't come easy and the hours are long. "It's not like you have a job from eight to five, eight hours a day, and then forget it," explains Carr. "If that is all that you are going to put into it, you're not going to get much out of it."

Ellwood Carr is living proof that you're never too old to learn. After years of successful farming, Carr and his wife, Ruth, left California to work as the farm managers of a mission school in a southeastern Kentucky coal mining area.

Before long, they moved atop a country store, where Carr was introduced to the world of herbs by laid-off coal miners who came to trade herbs for groceries. Since then, Carr has become an "herbal advocate," giving many lectures and workshops on edible wild plants and medicinal herbs.

Carr once used his herb expertise to historically document the edible flora of three downtown city blocks being razed for a parking lot in the city of Lexington. By making a makeshift kitchen and stationing himself at a table with pots and pans in hand, Carr pretended to be cooking for his supper the plants that he found in the vacant lots.

With a twinkle in his eye, Carr told passersby that this would be the last time that anyone would have the opportunity to gather and eat their supper in this location. From then on the land would be blacktopped. He made the local newspapers and his point was well taken. He came up with an inventory of more than 50 species that could be used for food—edible wild plants.

Ellwood J. Carr
Chenoa, Kentucky

Ellwood Carr

It is rather interesting when you change careers. You don't generally; a man is afraid, even at 45, to change his job. To fall into a creative situation is rather rare, like when my wife and I bought this little country store in Chenoa, Kentucky. But this is how I got into the whole world of medicinal plants and wild edible plants.

I was pretty near 50 and had been working as farm manager for the Henderson Settlement Methodist Mission in Bell County, Kentucky, close to where we live now. We left the mission after three years and bought a country store; that is, the bank bought it with a loan to us until we paid for it in twenty years. We felt that the mission was too isolated from the community. We had no private income and planned to use the store as a means of support and live in four small rooms over the store.

The original intention of the store was to use it as an access to the people in the community, and as a community center, which we have pretty much managed to do. The County Extension Homemakers clubs and various other groups, including vacation Bible school, meet in an extension to the store built for us by a volunteer group from Michigan several years ago. We know everybody around here and they know us; they come in for this, that, and the other thing. We distribute clothing, make helpful telephone calls. My wife helps people get advice, where to get legal aid and things like that.

Adjacent to the store I have an herbary. It's just a little concrete building 20 by 20. Recently I was taking an inventory of all my specimens. I have a display now of more than 300 different plant materials, used as medicinal herbs, and an equal number of specimens of edible wild plants, all fairly common here in Kentucky. They can be gathered and used at various times of the season. And then I have acquired an extensive library of books and clippings that I have used in writing my articles for the *Lexington Herald Leader*—some 450 over the past seven years. To illustrate the articles I have drawn heavily upon my collection of some 25,000 color slides, which I copied into black and white and printed the negatives. I wrote weekly articles on different types of nature subjects, mostly of plant life, their history, lore, the results of my experimentation and so forth. There is a growing interest in this kind of thing, and it is an inexhaustible resource; it just keeps growing in different directions.

It all happened in 1957, when we bought the store. The coal mines in the area had shut down and there was a lot of unemployment. People didn't have the government programs or the help that is available today for free. People brought in herbs that they gathered—ginseng, bloodroot, and so on—that they wanted either to sell or trade for groceries. I had no knowledge or conception of this subject whatsoever. So, at night, to satisfy my curiosity, I would dig through the *Encyclopedia Americana* and look up all the weird names of what they said these things were. Then I happened to run across an article in the encyclopedia on medicinal plants, and it just kind of "blew the lid off" things. After that I borrowed a three-volume set of *Britton & Brown Illustrated Flora* and began to collect plants that I would see, and to collect medicinal specimens to talk about with people who came into the store. It wasn't long before I had more medicinal plant specimens on my shelves than even these people had ever heard of. In order to make the identification of the plants, I would thumb through the 1,650 pages of this three-volume flora of the northeastern U.S. page by page, holding the plant in one hand until I found the plant. Sometimes, it would take three or four trips to find it, and sometimes I wouldn't find it at all, and end up in frustration, until after many months I learned plant-part terminology, and could run the plant down through the taxonomy key system.

My interest is in the wild medicinal plants, although I have made some interesting but dangerous inroads into my wife's flower garden, which is another story. In collecting I keep careful track of my time and try to go to areas where the herbs are plentiful. I don't waste time, but collect as though I were going to make a living at it. I also take account of my transportation time and cost so that if some time I would decide to buy the herbs that I would be interested in, I would know what they were worth. Many of my herbs are not listed in the wholesale catalogs. Also, I would want to be able to get them fresh, since some herbs lose their potency with age, some in as little as six months.

I had thought of starting an herb collecting cooperative so that in times of acute unemployment we could help people to help themselves. The idea of keeping track of the time for gathering the green herbs and the ratio of green to dry weight was so that we could pay people on a green weight basis. If a family needs groceries or money, it is not much help to have to wait a week or two until their herbs are dry to be able to sell them. Credit in a country store has bankrupted hundreds, and a bird in the hand is worth two in the bush, as they say—or rather an herb in the hand goes the same way. Then too, they might not do the drying properly. So, I have all these records worked back on an hourly basis as to what I could afford to pay.

Right now, I have 30 key herbs that I could gather,

package, and sell. We don't sell them in the store, but I keep them in my herbary. Since my retirement as a naturalist from National Audubon, my wife keeps the store and she is not inclined to take the space to stock them. In fact, people who come in the store today are not inclined to use such things. They have moved away from this. You're apt to get much more reception in herb shops, antique and curio shops than in these little country stores. To a great extent, country people have gotten away from herbs because of the government give-away programs—food stamps, allotments, and all that type of thing. It is easier, if they have a medical card, to just go to the doctor for every little ache and pain. However, many times they may have the root of their cure right in their own backyard, fence row, or in the woods behind the house. My wife has seen babies brought into the store with their mothers in hysterics, and the baby practically unconscious and white as a sheet, with nothing in the world wrong with the baby except worms. There are things that they could gather with the proper application that could prevent worms in the first place or expel them in aggravated conditions. Tansy, for example, could be used, and it was grown in country gardens for such purposes. Another plant that is a common weed around here that could be used is wormseed. Another name for it is Mexican tea.

Black lung is something that you hear more about with miners in the '40s and '50s. But for the relief of congestion or asthma, or something like that, you can drink mullein tea. The older generation used to smoke mullein leaves or jimson weed to open up their lungs and make it easier to breathe.

Of course, I don't prescribe or try to give things to people to take as medicine, although I have all the book information. My interest in herbs is more of an educational interest to remind people as to how at one time we were entirely dependent upon herb plants for medicine, and as far as that's concerned we still are. In my workshops I bring up the survival question. For example, what would you do if suddenly, say in an economic situation, everyone you know is unemployed and out of work? How could you care for yourself or your family? How could you even exist?

People are beginning to realize that there are means of survival. It is rather interesting that, out of all the plants on the face of the earth, 90 percent of human energy around the world comes from only 15 species of plants. In our own country, our vegetables come from rather geographically restricted areas, such as Florida and California, and what is lacking in those soils will be lacking in the urban diet in which these commercial vegetables are marketed. It seems obvious that the broader the intake of plant species and their geographic origin the more you are apt to maintain a good healthy body, with a better balance of trace minerals, vitamins, and enzymes, some of which you need in only very minute amounts, but they are essential to good health. One only needs to compare a chart of the analysis of wild edible plants compared to our cultivated plants to get some idea of the importance of considering food as medicine. Really, where do you draw the line between medicine and food? It is a pretty fine line when you get right down to it.

Today, many people are understandably afraid of some of the drugs the doctors are handing out. Partly because of this, many in the medical profession are beginning to come around to the point of saying, yes, there is a place for herb remedies, intelligently used. And, I think *intelligently* needs to be stressed. Few people can properly identify plants in the wild let alone administer them as medicine, even in their simplest uses. I stress this very carefully and emphatically at all of my workshops, because you have look-alikes and name similarities that may involve poisonous plants. You can get yourself into deep trouble if you don't know exactly what you are looking for, the parts used, the time for gathering them, and proper storage.

Many people in the low income classes have lost the incentive to do anything for themselves; they would rather "draw," as they call it, than work, and many who work in high paying jobs find excuses or deliberately work just enough to qualify for unemployment insurance. The coal mining people are earning $75 to $100 a day; about the only thing they will go out and gather now is ginseng, which sells for $100 to $120 a pound. Many can go out and gather half a pound a day if they can take off work, or go on sick leave. However, ginseng is something that not everyone is going to find. For the average person going out into the woods to find ginseng, it probably would be a week before they even found one root. Ginseng hunters have their favorite haunts, and they keep going back over these areas periodically. It is not a plentiful plant to find under the best of circumstances. With the excessively high prices being offered by the oriental exporters ginseng is becoming an endangered species throughout the eastern part of the U.S. where it is native.

It is interesting, the type of people you meet working as a naturalist and in conducting workshops in edible wild plants and medicinal herbs. I was doing a wild plant foods workshop at the Buckley Wildlife Sanctuary near Frankfort and only about 20 miles from the University of Kentucky. Believe me, 25 years ago teaching these people about plants would have been the farthest thing from my mind. Anyway, there were a lot of the "far left" group there, and it was amazing since they were the ones who utilized the sanctuary. They came out and walked the trails with me, and seemed to hang on every word I had to say.

At the first wild plant foods workshop I gave, I had only three people who were brave enough to sample the foods.

But at the fourth annual one that I gave in 1975, I had over 60 different plant food dishes to offer in ten different categories. It was a complete dinner in courses. There were about 250 people who attended the two-day affair. The kids from the University of Kentucky about swamped the place. An hour before we opened the back door for them to come in, they were lined up two abreast clear back to the parking lot a hundred feet away. I just had no idea that the edible wild plant thing would strike that much interest.

Of course, this type of thing isn't for everybody. Lots of people just aren't interested. Oh, if the seed comes from Ferry-Morse and you have to plow the ground, plant it, hoe it, fertilize it, and then chase the birds away and keep the ground hogs out, my wife will eat those plants. But, this thing of getting plants to eat from the weed patch or fence row, well she isn't inclined to that kind of thing at all. So, about the only opportunity that I have for cooking these things is when I put on one of my workshops or experiment on my own to create a recipe for some new plant. As far as home cooking is concerned, my diet is what's put before me, and that is the customary food that's cooked and prepared from the garden or the store. My wife is an avid gardener, so it makes her a little upset when she gardens all spring and summer, and finally in the fall the weeds take over. That's when I go out in the garden and gather up all the good things out there that she calls weeds. I tell her, "Gee whiz, you've missed a lot of good things out there." Really, a garden is a good place for foraging.

Today my wife takes care of the store entirely. I hardly even enter into it. That's because this wild plant foods and medicinal herb thing has become a full-time hobby for me. It's a hobby, yes, but it's a little more serious than a hobby. I utilize it in this sense. I'm kind of free to go here and there and develop whatever comes up, but then again, I'm responsible for the programs that I develop. It's not like you have a job from eight to five, eight hours a day, and then forget it. If that is all that you are going to put into it, you're not going to get much out of it.

Considering how I have gotten into this type of work, and how it developed step by step over the years since leaving California, I feel that the Lord Almighty has had a hand in it. And, I have always had a philosophy of hanging loose, as it were, so that I could be easily moved by the Spirit.

I'm in my early 70s, and I still feel that I am being prepared for something else. I don't know what it is; I'll leave that up to the Lord—I'm counting on it having something to do with plants—I'm pretty sure of that.

Born in Seattle, *Carolyn Hutchinson* has lived on both coasts. After her own health broke down, Hutchinson became involved with medicinal herbs. She began studying herbs everywhere she went and opened small herb stores wherever she made her home.

An energetic woman who welcomes her patrons with open arms, Carolyn is pleased with the success of her latest venture in Spring Lake, Michigan. Although she enjoys the local trade, it wasn't always so. Some members of the conservative community at first thought of herbalism as witchcraft. But as people attended her herbal classes and lectures, that image dissipated. Her shop's approach is strictly nutritional, through the use of whole herbs and food.

Carolyn Hutchinson
Spring Lake, Michigan

Carolyn Hutchinson

In some ways, it all started when my husband changed jobs. He was hired as an engineer by a company in Worcester, Massachusetts. Before that, we had been living in Connecticut. Frankly, this was probably the only way I would have ever given up teaching music. I loved it. If you're worth your salt in that particular field, and you give it your all, well, it's just about impossible to leave it. You always have a younger student coming along. Johnny has a sister who's been waiting until age 8 for lessons. Parents say, "You can't possibly leave us now." The only way I could have left that career and gotten into the herb business was through a major move.

When we got to Massachusetts, I began with a store, or, quite literally, a closet in my home, called The Sweet Leaf. I had this walk-in closet with little shelves and jars that probably contained at least 100 different kinds of herbs. That would have been about 1974. I didn't know for sure what I was going to do, but I figured I might as well make a full-time commitment to herbs, since Worcester already had enough piano teachers. But, of course, business was very slow with such a small operation.

After about three months in my home, and very little traffic, I got up my nerve and started writing a health column. I volunteered myself to a weekly newspaper and called it, "Sarsaparilla and Sage," incorporating a lot of recipes, fasting, and cleansing information. By this time in my life I had built up quite a storehouse of information about herbs and herbal remedies. Once I had been real sick and healed myself with herbs.

Anyway, shortly after we got to Massachusetts, and I found out that my closet wasn't going to do the trick, I took the big step of renting a storefront in the adjacent town of Leicester. I still used the name Sweet Leaf, but this time I plunged right into it. My first few days, I can remember my sales were about $3 a day. The first time I sold $30, I thought the world had absolutely fallen on my doorstep. I figured that at $30, and with a very small over-head, I could just about cover my rent and utilities. I heated the store with sunshine and, fortunately, we had sunshine almost every day. Except for our winter storms, that lasted maybe 12 hours, we had gorgeous sunshine. The largest heating bill I ever had was $11 per month. I think my rent was $110. So the $30 a day meant I was going to make it. It was definitely a struggle. But within three months I went into the black.

In setting up my own business, a store that had a tre-mendous influence on me was called The Good Food Store, in Connecticut. It was a natural foods store, much like my own is today. I don't believe they carried any vitamins, but they had one whole wall of herbs, and everything was in bulk. The whole front yard was solid sunflowers—a neat place in an old house and I loved to go there. It was a real grassroots type of thing, with basic whole foods, herbs, juices, and reference books. I took it with me as my inspiration when we moved.

Just like the Good Food Store, I put an emphasis on medicinal herbs, books, and natural foods. I soon learned that the bigger my inventory, the easier it was to sell. So the more I expanded, the easier it got. After three years things were really rolling well, and the store had a good reputation. But that was just about the time my husband had a job transfer, and we ended up here in the little town of Spring Lake, Michigan.

Oh, I wanted so badly to do it again. I packed up my jars, shelves, and the counter in the herb room and I recycled everything here. I started out in an antique store. I was given one room rent-free if, in return, I would manage the shop. It sounded ideal, but what happened was that this isn't a great area for antiques. Frugal, conservative, wintertime, there's nothing going on. The traffic was very low, and before I knew it, I was back to the $3 a day again. After six months, I realized that I couldn't justify the amount of time I spent without any real income. So I packed up my herbs and carted them back home again. For two years, my die-hard customers would come to my garage for herbs.

By the time I finally got it together to open a real store, I changed the name to The Village Grain Station. I knew I would have to sell more than just herbs in western Michigan. This time I would be carrying a line of natural foods, I would have a real store.

At first the idea of having a shop at your home may appear convenient, but you have no separation between your work and home. Your private hours are not apt to be honored. And there is this psychological thing that people don't take you seriously unless you have a storefront. You've got to take a risk and go out on a limb.

I try to keep my overhead low. You don't need as big a store space as you think. About 800 square feet is enough. And you don't have to be on a main street for the walk-in trade. The people who want chamomile will seek you out. In the beginning, keep it small; that way your utilities can be kept to a minimum.

What really makes people keep coming back to my store is the satisfaction of knowing that they're really being helped. And listening with a third ear is the best way to do

this. My approach is low key and involves kitchen remedies. I establish my integrity with someone by giving them
a chunk of my time without making a sale.

People are on all levels in this community. They have
different fears of things that they don't know about.
There's certainly a degree of fearfulness about something
that has the reputation that herbs do in being connected
with witches and the occult. Spring Lake is a beautifully
religious community, but at the same time there are people who are so conservative in their outlooks. It's under-
standable in a way, since herbs have always been somewhat mysterious until recently, when we've been able to
isolate the properties, and say there are so many parts of
calcium salts in this and so many potassium salts in
chamomile tea and so forth. Now we can explain that
that's why a certain herb is a sedative to the nerves. Before, people would drink the tea and not know why it
worked, so really the mystery was the witchery part of it.
Herbs had this reputation of working in ways that no one
understood.

Despite the fears and superstitions around here, there
are new faces in my store every day. I think there's been
such a need. Every third person who comes tells me,
"Thanks for doing this. We needed it."

If I only sold herbs, I'd have to ask for donations to keep
the store going. But there is one product that pays the
rent—"gorp" or trail mix. The nuts and the trail mix are
big sellers, and I have steady traffic for those items. Other
staples such as oatmeal and peanut butter also help.
Whether or not we like it, carrying popular food items gets
people in the door and keeps them coming back. I'd advise starting out slowly to develop a bond of trust. And I
make commitments in other ways than through the store.
I give lectures and classes to service groups and clubs. A
lot are free, but I feel I'm doing something for the community.

It's important to set up the food in an attractive, self-service manner. This saves a tremendous amount of your own labor. I'd suggest investing in a good digital scale that weighs to ⅙ of an ounce. I've purchased a Hobart scale for about $1,500. In the beginning I was bagging items about four hours a day and always at the end of a scoop. But the Hobart frees you to help those who really need your help.

My store is very non-threatening as a food store. It's good to advertise a little when you first open up. That helps people get to know you. Then, once you get established, you can cut it off a bit. I spend about $200 a month for advertising. I've found that the "Notices" section of the classifieds produces good results. It's much cheaper than a display ad, and I usually feature one product. Another good idea is to make up flyers and pay the newspaper boys to drop them off, or leave them in banks and libraries. I've even paid members of my family to take them around.

Presently, I'm sponsoring a portion of a classical and jazz program on a local PBS radio station. Public broadcasting costs me $10 per week. They simply say, "this program has been made possible by the Village Grain Station of Spring Lake, purveyors of natural foods." From this I can claim a double tax deduction from a nonprofit organization and receive a break on my state income tax. Underwriting on PBS is lots cheaper than advertising on local radio stations.

A lending library and lending tapes is another goodwill idea. I'd like to offer books to people who need information without forcing them to buy a book; I like to let them know what health books are available in the library. This is part of the health education process. It lets people know that I'm not in this for the money.

One thing I want to learn more about is how to gather my own herbs. But so far, I'm just not comfortable with it. Foraging is a big responsibility. Fortunately, I have some excellent suppliers who import directly: Sweethardt Herbs, Green Mountain, San Francisco Herb Company. These are just a few. I guess I feel that as long as I'm on a retail level and I have suppliers to fall back on, it's a kind of security blanket.

Rapid service is a must. To get the herbs I need I just call a toll-free number with my order, and within four days UPS delivers it. This way, I can keep my inventory fairly low. And then, if someone comes in and asks for something rare that I might not have, I can come up with a $50 or $100 minimum order in 10 minutes. I just make a call, and within a few days I have the herb the customer wants.

I've never felt that I received stale herbs. But one of the secrets is to get the herbs out of the sun and into jars. Shelves and glass jars can be a considerable investment. And it helps to shelve the medicinal herbs near the culinary ones. That way I have no bug problem because the bugs don't like the smell of mints, bay leaves, or cayenne. No one likes to talk about it, but you could have a real disaster with bugs; you might have to throw out pounds and pounds of stock. Another factor for keeping out bugs involves keeping the store cool. I wear layers of sweaters all day, but the customers aren't uncomfortable because they come in here in their winter coats.

At first, I would advise against purchasing a cooler. It's really a loss because it won't pay for itself unless you have regular customers who purchase the eggs, tofu, milk, and so on. Because a cooler takes a lot of electricity, I'd advise doing without one for a year. Build up your business first. New coolers cost about $2,000. I waited eight months and purchased a used cooler for $400.

My husband still tells me that if I get smart I'll start selling vitamins to make a little money. And I can hardly blame him, because without his income I wouldn't be able to run the store the way I do. I understand how people make compromises when they're forced to get their living out of the store. You have to survive.

My biggest problem is time. I don't have enough time. I'm there six days a week, and I still get people who want me to open up earlier. I have to keep my goods simple. Even now, there is no money in my business for employees. My business is either self-run or family run. The paper work would be tremendous, with workman's compensation, federal and state unemployment compensation, and Social Security. The more employees, the more paper work.

You simply can't count on living off the store for at least two years. You should plan ahead or have a working spouse or some other form of income if you want to start your own store. And you've got to learn not to be greedy to make big sales. I've learned all these things through the school of hard knocks. My first store in Massachusetts was a real learning experience. I started too low then, with a capital outlay of $500, and I ended up selling air. It's best to borrow some money and have enough in the store to be able to please people. My customers there were patient; they grew with me.

Now that I've finally got a real business underway, I have managed to bring some of my music back. I picked up a $50 piano and put it in my store. And that's the best investment I've made so far. If music is your thing, get a stereo. There's no way you can get a lunch break. If the snow comes down and I'm all alone and snowed in, I sit down and play my piano. It makes even a slow day special.

CHAPTER FIVE

How Herbs Grow

ALTHOUGH THEY are often called weeds, herbs are the oldest, the most persistent, and perhaps the most stylish of all the cultivated garden species. In every culture, herbs are listed among the earliest of the domestically grown foods and medicines.

Not until the sixth century, however, did the art of formal herb gardening come into its own. That's when St. Benedict (patron saint of the Benedictines) came upon a novel idea to help the monks of Monto Cassino become self-supporting. St. Benedict's idea, which was designed to help establish the first communal-living order within the church, consisted of growing herbs in rectangular beds with low brick or board facings. His success was astounding. His model garden formed the pattern for similar monastic plots throughout Europe for the next 1,000 years.

Notwithstanding the practicality of St. Benedict's designs, after ten centuries his humble gardens had evolved into the most intricate patterns conceivable. Appropriately called conceits or knot gardens, these elaborate patterns were the products of sixteenth-century European noblemen, who employed skilled architects to twist the herb plantings into ropelike rows of grays and greens. The overall impact was at once as highly impractical as it was

157

fashionable. The fad lasted but a short time, with the exception of specialized and historical gardens.

Fortunately, all was not lost to style. The same period saw the origins of the first botanic garden, when in 1545, an Italian professor decided to supply his colleagues with needed herbs and medicines. Professor Bonafede's tidy design's worked well, and even today his exquisitely tiered gardens serve as inspiration for thousands of visitors to the university gardens at Padua.

The "fashionable weeds" made a return to formal gardening in England and France in the seventeenth century, when herbs were shaped into fanciful parterre gardens. Most peculiarly, these gardens were designed to be seen but not necessarily walked in by their aristocratic owners. Trimmed into living embroideries, the parterre gardens spread out in stunning patterns beneath the high windows of regal estates and palaces. Made to appear as if they were growing extensions of rugs and tapestries, when viewed from above the perfectly manicured hedges formed what appeared to be identical replicas of their indoor counterparts. To create such stunning effects, the darker embroidery patterns of the hedges were made to contrast sharply with white spaces of carefully raked sand.

Present-day developments of the parterre gardens can be found in formal herb gardens, as well as in more ordinary civic gardens, where plantings are designed to be viewed from towering skyscrapers rather than from the palaces of days gone by.

Although the gardens of *Louis Saso* and *Kathi Keville* are very much designed to be walked in, touched, smelled, and enjoyed, Saso and Keville are keeping tradition alive not only in the way of design—as evidenced by Saso's zodiac garden—but also with their insistence on replacing modern methods with organic gardening. Their productive farms are ample evidence that small-scale organic herb farms can be largely, if not wholly, self-supporting.

In the foothills of Northern California's Sierra Nevadas, *Kathi Keville* owns and operates the Oak Valley Herb Farm, where wild and cultivated herbs are grown, gathered, and made into lotions, teas, and salves.

A former Girl Scout, Keville looks like "the girl next door"—clear complexion, glistening eyes, and a bright, glowing smile. Keville joined the Herb Society of America while studying art at California State University, Long Beach, and soon was growing and collecting her own herbs. She moved to Oak Valley with a box of potted herbs from her garden. She asked the manager where the herb garden was and he replied, "I think it just arrived."

The herb garden was planted, and Keville learned the fine art of herb growing, soil maintenance, harvesting, and herbal preparation.

Oak Valley has served as an inspirational model for many in the herbal community. Through herb walks and seminars, Oak Valley seeks to introduce people to an appreciation of herbs through their beauty and healthful qualities.

Kathi Keville
Oak Valley, California

Kathi Keville

I'm always weeding, planting, composting, drying flowers, taking a picture of herbs, or working on one of the many other things which need to be done around here. Being an herb farmer requires a tremendous amount of work.

We're here to help others with herb walks and classes, but if you come by just for a visit, you might end up with a shovel in your hands.

The main thing we do is cultivate the herbs, mix and bag teas, prepare body care products and bottle them, and glue on lots of labels. The whole thing takes a long time and helps me realize why people invented machines, although I am really glad to not be using any.

We do have a roto tiller, but the garden was originally "double dug," and we went for years without one. When we finally accepted the fact that one was needed to deal with the hard clay soil, it came as a real blessing. It has helped us expand quite a bit. There are two acres cultivated with 300 different varieties of herbs and another 75 wild herbs in the forests and meadows.

The business is small, which allows us to maintain the high quality. People usually find out about us just by word of mouth. We're so small, in fact, that we really can't be competitive. It may sound strange, but actually I wouldn't mind if everyone eventually just stopped buying our products and started making their own.

I like to use both domestic and wild herbs in the products. Certainly the cultivated herbs are very strong and they serve the same purposes as the wild ones, but I think you sometimes develop a greater affinity for the herbs which grow right around you. They're growing out of the same soil you walk on and they're breathing the same air. It's a kind of "macrobiotic" idea of herbology.

Actually, the way I grow herbs, they're in a semi-wild state even in the garden. First of all, I look to the area where the plant originated, to get a feel for its own environment, and then adapt it somewhat. I try to find out if it grew in the Mediterranean, in sandy soil—like thyme, rosemary—or if it comes from a humid area such as Michigan—sassafras and ginseng. Because the herbs have not been highly hybridized in the way vegetables have, they adapt very well to growing in different climates. They're very strong and hearty. Eventually, I hope to make little sub-environments with greenhouses so that I can grow an even wider variety. That way visitors can see how many different plants there are without having to travel all around the world.

Since there is such a short growing season in the Sierra, I have to put the herbs to bed for the winter, and, frankly, each year I wonder if they're going to come up or not. By late fall and into early spring, it's pretty barren in the garden. And then, all of a sudden, herbs start shooting up, and I'm out there crawling around on hands and knees, all excited and saying, "Oh, here's one! Oh, the pineapple sage is coming back, and look over there!" Then, pretty soon, the self-seeding annuals appear and everything's underway. Actually, the herb garden just comes up on its own. I can keep the potted herbs, which I sell during the summer, in the lath house all winter. The tops die down just like they do in the ground, and then in the spring, I start watering them and up they come.

The soil, which is basically very, very heavy clay, needs

a lot of work. We've had to get granite sand from the cliffs to aerate the soil. Also the soil is very acidic. Compost enriches it and brings it back to neutral. You can really see the difference between the herb beds and the pathways. The beds have changed to a deep brown color, but the regular soil is still red. The red is good because it means the soil has lots of nutrients and holds water, but many herbs don't like to have their roots wet. In every case we have to look at their natural environment to see how they prefer it. Sometimes they like shade or maybe sun or lots of water or maybe not very much water at all. We have to treat them right. There is a vegetable garden, but I grow herbs in it also. Sometimes I can't really tell the difference. I use them both for food and medicine.

We read about herbs having certain alkaloids or essential oils. It's fascinating to find out what these are and how they work in the body. Through modern medicine we can begin to understand why herbs sometimes work on certain people and why they sometimes don't work. We are able for the first time to combine the old herbal knowledge with scientific insights and understand a very total picture. Not only is the chemistry in people's bodies different, but the chemistry in the herbs can fluctuate according to how they're grown. Depending on the soil, water, and sun, they can pick up different nutrients.

There are a lot of reasons why an herb does not have an effect on someone. It's hard to generalize. Many times the herbs are poor quality. But people can always tell if they have good herbs just by using their eyes to see if the color is still there and their nose to check if the fragrance is strong. When you go into a health foods store or an herb shop, if the herb is black it's been improperly dried or stored. It probably has lost its important properties.

Many stores cannot obtain quality herbs. You find stem instead of leaf and very little fragrance. That is why I grow so many herbs and encourage others to do the same. And it is the best way to be sure they are not sprayed. When you copy a formula from an herb book and use the same proportions with store-bought herbs, you'll possibly have a weaker product than intended. People don't realize that most herbalists traditionally use herbs from their own garden or the wild.

There's a whole seasonal thing that happens with herbs. In the winter, they hold their energy and also most of their properties in the roots. And then, early in the spring, when they begin to throw their first shoots up, the energy starts to rise. That's a good time to decide whether or not you want to use the root because most of the nutrients will be there until the leaves are fully out. Herbs that are picked mainly for the leaves are picked just before the flower comes. But once the herbs blossom, the vitality goes to the flowers. You'll begin to see the leaves dropping and turning yellow. Sometimes the insects will come, and you will just know that the lower leaves aren't good medicine anymore. That's the time to pick the flowers. In the fall the seeds come and the whole cycle is completed. After the seeds fall back to the ground, the perennials will return their energy to the roots. In late fall, the roots can be dug. They'll last all winter and will give you really good, strong teas.

This corresponds with the way we eat because in the winter we're eating heavier foods. Seeds and many roots are high in carminatives, which help with digestion. And then, early in the spring, we can take the "blood purifier" roots like burdock root and sassafras to clean out our winter sluggishness.

Rolling Thunder and other American Indian medicine people have demonstrated some beautiful ceremonies. He showed me how to find the grandfather plant in a patch. Once you find it, you go and ask it if the others may be taken. Then you leave it alone and don't pick it.

I don't have a specific ritual that I go through, and I

always feel that it doesn't really matter much. You don't have to get down on your hands and knees and talk to the plant—it's just what you feel in your heart. When you have the love and dedication to work with the herbs in a good way, that's all it takes.

When I first started studying herbs in 1970, it wasn't nearly as popular as it is now—I had to search for people who understood them. I wanted to find out what part was just "folklore" and what part was real. Of course, I'm still learning. The garden has been my primary teacher. Every time I add a little to my knowledge about herbs, I realize there's so much more. Every time I open a new door, there are so many more doors, and I realize there is much more than I could possibly learn in a lifetime. I'm just glad I got started as early as I did.

Louis Saso's garden is a very special place, a peaceful sanctuary amid the suburban spread of the south San Francisco Bay area. Always experimenting, Saso has used the French Intensive Method and the Rodale method, as well as his own.

After 25 years of growing culinary herbs, Saso now organically grows plants for medicinal purposes and stresses that it's very important *how* an herb is grown. He uses entirely organic sprays in combination with companion planting.

A healthy looking man with a gentle nature, Saso believes that his acquired knowledge of growing herbs is important in this age because the vibrant plants can be used to fortify people's health and to teach people about survival.

Louis Saso

People have to learn where their food is coming from and how it's grown. I know, I was in the produce business for 25 years before I got into herbs, and my family was in the produce business before that. I guess I was about 13 years old when my folks moved to San Jose and set up a market. In those days the health food stores were few and far between. The big stores, like the Safeways we have now, were taking over; I actually grew up in a dying business.

About 25 years ago I started to grow herbs so we would be able to keep our business. By that time I was married, and over the years we had had eight children. So to be successful in business, I felt we had to specialize. At first we grew herbs just for spices and cooking. You didn't hear much in those days about using herbs for tea or for healing. Of course, long before that people were using these same herbs for healing. People used many herbs for helping digestion of food, or maybe sage to help preserve meat. But gradually most people had come to think of herbs as seasonings.

In recent years, people became more aware of the medicinal side of it when they became conscious of the side effects of modern medicine. Then they started looking for alternatives. People were really searching for a better way. They tried drugs and a lot of different things but eventually they saw something better in herbs.

It's interesting when I look back (I'm well into my 60s now, and I've gone through changes in my lifetime). The

Louis Saso
San Francisco, California

whole world has changed so drastically, but I can see some of the good things that have happened.

Today we sell lots of herbs in the Santa Cruz area in natural foods stores and restaurants, and to people who are planting community and neighborhood gardens. I take pride in the fact that we're different from anyone else who is doing this commercially. I use all organic substances in my soil. It's actually a living type of soil, made out of different manures and nutrients. Right now, I'm experimenting with worm castings, which are one of the very best of all fertilizers. It's really just leaves, compost that the worms have turned into food for plants. It's one of the very best. Plants and people are the same in a lot of ways. If they are fed well and kept healthy, they are just going to be stronger. My herbs might have twice the potency of an herb that's grown in poor soil. See the difference?

We're always experimenting and doing different things in our garden. But I see proof of the value of our labors all the time. We use the artemisias and other bitter herbs to help repel insects. The artemisias give off various oils that help the soil. In a way they're like antibiotics and disinfectants for the soil. The marigold is another plant that helps repel the little wireworms in the soil. Farmers used to use wild mustard greens the same way. All of these things can help to kill or ward off harmful bacteria and insects.

When we have to spray, we use a garlic combination with cayenne pepper and soap. It works for white flies, aphids, and other harmful insects. The garlic fumes help repel the insects, and cayenne pepper works as the insects walk on it. I always tell people that the pepper gives the insects hot foot—they kind of lick their legs. You can use the pepper on ant trails or wherever there are crawling insects. I don't know if it kills them or not but it sure gets rid of them. The soap suds coat the leaves so the sucking insects can't damage the plant. I use a soap like Fels Naptha that has a kind of lye in it. I've found it effective.

But I always warn people that nothing is 100 percent effective because we can't change the balance of nature. Maybe it'll work at a 70 or 80 percent level, but it won't get rid of everything. I've often thought to myself, if we got rid of all the aphids, then we wouldn't have the ladybugs for which they are food. So what we always try to work with is the natural balance. If we can get enough insect predators and enough food for the predators, we'll keep our balance. We're definitely not going to get rid of all the things that are called undesirable. People get so unhappy with moles, but moles have their place in nature. They get rid of a lot of the insects in our garden. If we got rid of all the moles, we'd be so overrun with insects they would be worse than moles. Everything helps in the balance.

We have herbs in our garden from all over the world. We visited gardens in Europe—at the Chelsea Gardens in London and at the herb gardens in Padua, Italy, as well as many herb gardens in the U.S. A friend of mine collects seeds from several botanical gardens of the world, and he sends them to me. The last few years, I've gotten so many different varieties, I can't keep up with them.

We're lucky that our Saratoga area is adaptable to a lot of plants. I have lemon grass from Mexico that grows just like our local grass does. Lemon verbena is another one that does pretty well, but it's hard to propagate. The seeds need about a 90°F temperature to germinate. Then, there are some plants that just don't want to be moved from their home area at all. I found one that's quite difficult and grows wild quite close to here.

A couple of fellows I know found a spikenard ginseng (*Arailia californica*) plant, similar to ginseng, down in a deep ravine in the Santa Cruz Mountains and brought it to me. At first it did real well. And then, in the middle of summer, it started to die back. The insects really devoured that plant, and I thought, I've lost it. It just wasn't time for it to become dormant like that. But then, in spring, the plant came back. I was really surprised. I never sprayed it because I didn't want to.

In the same area I had some gota kola growing. I tried to set up an environment for that plant that would be like that in its native growing habitat. In India, it just grows wild. So I set up a small lath house in real deep soil. Because ginseng grows wild in maple forests, I tried to get maple leaf molds and some sawdust that was years and years old. I dug down a couple of feet and tried to get everything just like it would be in the field. But, still, the gota kola is very difficult. The leaves turn kind of brown, and I know now that that plant just doesn't want to be changed. I am using compost with worm castings as well as liquid fish emulsion and getting very good results.

My astrological herb garden is doing really well. The plants in it are growing just tremendously big. There is a lot of energy there. I'm still working on it. The center area, the round circle, is the sun area and then the other parts are the sun's rays. It's all done organically. We took out all the old soil and replaced it with leaves and compost and all the minerals I've been talking about. Most of the time, I've found that I don't need to fertilize if I have a healthy soil. I believe in earthworms working the soil and the energy of the sun. That's what makes your soil come alive.

In growing herbs, you have to experiment. Companion planting is one of the big factors. We're learning things constantly. We don't have to use poisons. We just have to be willing to experiment. It takes time.

We have been teaching workshops on organic gardening and the history, culture, and use of culinary, medicinal, and decorative herbs for over eight years. We use our herb gardens as one gigantic laboratory. Our classes are held in the spring and summer of each year. In this way, we hope to reach as many people as possible and introduce them to the fascinating world of herbs.

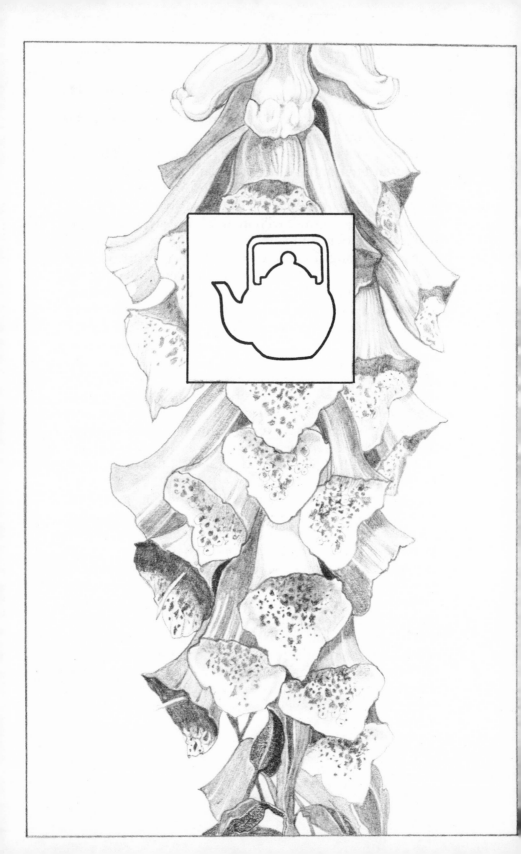

CHAPTER SIX

How To Use Herbs

Plants have been used for healing since the dawn of medical history, but only in the last two centuries have scientific methods been applied to their use. It is to phytochemical analysis, or in other words the process of isolating an herb's active principles, that modern medicine owes a great debt. From cinchona (Peruvian) bark came quinine, from opium emerged morphine, from ipecacuanha came emetine, and so on.

For the sake of efficiency and economics, pharmaceutical research workers generally look for those plant compounds that are fairly easily isolated and crystallized. We find today that a high percentage of the active principles isolated from plants are in the form of the nitrogen-containing compounds known as alkaloids. For example, the active principles obtained from ephedra, catharanthus, cinchona, belladonna, and many more, are all alkaloids. Often neglected in drug manufacturing are other useful, but harder to isolate herbal properties, such as steroids, iridoids, triperpenes, glycosides, and even antibiotics.

173

Foxglove

Most herbalists make a major distinction between a manufactured drug and the natural form on which its design is based. Generally, they argue that even when a pharmaceutically produced drug is chemically identical to an herb's active ingredients, it lacks the herb's "balancing" factors. Additional properties, found in the herb are seen as enhancing the active ingredients, providing valuable nutrients, and protecting against possible overdoses.

A revealing story involves the life, times, and transformation of foxglove into digitalis. Foxglove was first introduced to conventional medical practice in the late eighteenth century by Dr. William Withering, of Midland, England. According to Withering's account, he had stopped to change horses at a rural village when he was asked to help a woman suffering from dropsy, a condition caused by various heart disorders, as well as problems with the blood and lymph systems. In Withering's initial opinion, little could be done. Some weeks later, however, he happened to see the woman, and to his amazement she had virtually recovered.

Upon questioning the woman, he discovered that she had been seeing a village herbalist who recommended teas made from foxglove. From his extensive studies of the herb, Withering derived digitalis, which is formulated from the seeds and leaves of the plant. But even at the time, he warned his enthusiastic colleagues about possible adverse side effects when the heart-saving medication was given in either very large or repeated dosages.

Today, more than two centuries later, digitalis—or digoxin, as it is called in its most common synthetic form— is one of the most popular and valuable, as well as one of the potentially riskiest of all drugs used by cardiologists. In 1980, 23 million prescriptions were written in the United States alone for digitalis and its synthesized derivatives.

In the evolution of foxglove, much is said about the

impact of science on traditional herbal treatments. On the one hand, quantitative measurements of objective data have successfully replaced superstition and subjective impressions. On the other hand, giving digitalis in large and repeated dosages has increased the risks proportionately. Interestingly, today's side effects from overdosage remain much the same as those described by Dr. Withering, including abnormal heart beats, slackened pulse, vomiting, cold sweats, convulsions, and possibly death.

Among those herbalists on the leading edge of the battle to unite scientific fact with herbal wisdom is *Dr. James A. Duke,* who heads the Germplasm Resources Laboratory of the U.S. Department of Agriculture. Duke's efforts to track down possible cancer cures by systematically exploring the world's plant kingdom have met with some surprising results. According to Duke, one out of ten plants selected for serious study appears in the preliminary testing stages to have some effect on cancer.

Stan Malstrom's interest in plants is also linked with his early work on a cancer research project. Malstrom, however, left this conventional research to study the nutritional aspects of herbs. Prevention, Malstrom feels, is the key to solving the problem of cancer.

Beyond medicinal and nutritional uses, herbs can prove beneficial on more subtle levels. *Norma Myers* warns us that no matter how we use herbs we must use them knowingly, respectfully, and sparingly. Whatever our needs, herbs represent a renewable but still limited resource.

As chief of the Medicinal Plant Resources Laboratory, now part of the Germplasm Resources Laboratory of the U.S. Department of Agriculture, *James A. Duke* hunted down rare plants for the National Cancer Institute. In his quests, Duke has traveled far, leading plant gathering expeditions to Mexico, Panama, Syria, Honduras, China, and Egypt.

A tall, robust man with a distinct Southern drawl, Duke admits to experiments with herbs for his own health problems, but he cautions others to become properly educated in their use of herbs. He notes that certain herbs which can be purchased over the counter could be harmful or conceivably even fatal. To help promote more reliable standards for professionals and consumers, Duke's office is developing computerized data banks on medicinal plants throughout the world. An entry consists of five columns: scientific name, common name, use, locality, and source. To date, more than 88,000 plants have been listed.

James A. Duke

I started out at 16 as a blue grass fiddler, even making it to the Grand Ole Opry, and kept an interest in plants on the side. But later on, I acquired a Ph.D. in botany from the University of North Carolina, and the fiddling went more to the side. Presently, I'm head of the Germplasm Resources Laboratory of the U.S. Department of Agriculture, which in a sense means I'm one of the federal government's chief herb testers.

One of my biggest concerns now is trying to track down plant sources of possible cancer cures. The National Cancer Institute (NCI) has already gone through more than 10 percent of the plants in the world. And, most gratifyingly, nearly one extract in ten seems to have some effect on cancer, at least in the test tube stage. The real potential lies in the hundreds of plants ahead, the ones that have never been tested, and maybe even have not been discovered so far.

The superstar of plants, for anticancer activity, is Madagascar periwinkle, *Catharanthus roseus*. It's the source of two compounds called vincristine and vinblastine

James A. Duke
Beltsville, Maryland

which have proven remarkably effective in combination with conventional chemotherapy. For example, it helps produce an 80 percent remission rate in Hodgkin's disease, 90 percent in leukemia, and 80 percent in Wilm's tumor.

Since we've been through only about 10 percent of the plant kingdom, does this mean there are nine more superstars waiting? If we screened all the plants in the world, would we find some equally good or better? On a hunch, I would say that there are at least five more superstars waiting for us, possibly in some materials I brought back from China.

More and more, we're moving our searches into the rain forests, largely because they've been somewhat neglected in our cancer program to date. But the hardest part of working in these places is drying the plants. If you don't get them dried out, all you bring back is a bunch of mildew. Presently, we're working on new ways of packing them, such as in alcohol. But the potential is superb because the rain forests not only possess the greatest number of plants, but they also have the most diversified species, many of them narrowly endemic.

We're concentrating on the forests in the Americas now because prior concentrations of our program were primarily in Africa. We're looking especially to rain forests in Bolivia, Brazil, Colombia, Ecuador, and Venezuela.

When we go to places like these, we're most interested, not only in medical plants generally, but also in the poisonous ones. It seems strange but it takes poison to fight poison, and the poisonous plants are most likely to show some antitumor activity in the cancer program. We're interested in both the positive and the negative effects.

If we happen to encounter a good witch doctor, the first thing we ask for is his poisonous plants; then we ask for his medicinal remedies. If we don't have our bags full by then, we'll go for anything else we can describe. Our highest priority is to get new plant families, genera, or species to the NCI; i.e., taxa they have never screened before. How to name it can be a problem. Usually, we have to get the specimens with flowers and fruits, but so many of them have never been identified. In terms of resources, we'll try to check with both the witch doctor and the area botanist. Botanists vary tremendously, but if you find one who is an ethnobotanist, which is what I call myself, he'll be interested in the relationship of plants and people. The witch doctor will know which plants are potent, and if I can persuade him to tell me, I'll know which ones to bring back home.

For example, when I was in Panama, we found two Indian cultures that were very different. The Choco and the Cuna. The Choco were forest people who had acquired an extensive repertoire of local medicinal herbs. They were very different from the Cuna Indians, who were, shall we say, "city slickers." The Cuna congregated in villages as opposed to the Choco, who were scattered about one family per mile along the river. The river was the only highway. The Cuna used every plant available. To their way of thinking, God had put everything here with a meaning, and they used not only all of the plants but rocks and broken records, pieces of crucifixes, or even broken glass or other objects. All this would be thrown into pulverized mixtures, which might be taken either as a bath or internally.

The Choco, on the other hand, were very specific in their applications. You would find only one or two herbs in a concoction. I tried a couple of them myself, one was a toothache bush, which worked quite well, and then I took several of their teas.

In learning about their medicine I would go to both the Choco and the Cuna witch doctors. The witch doctors of both tribes are highly respected, but they tend to dislike each other intensely. So, first I would ask a Choco how he used his plants and then I would tell him, "Ah, that's the plant the Cuna used for such and such." The Choco would then reply—something like, "Bah, humbug, the Cuna don't know what they're talking about." And then he would tell me his own remedies. It was a way of allowing them to volunteer the information rather than having to pull it out of them. I believe it worked. I think I got most of the information.

I've been traveling around the tropics for over 25 years, and no trip is more difficult than a cancer "collecting trip." We must collect three pounds of dry weight per sample. In some cases, it takes days to collect this much. We also must be very careful not to endanger any rare species. We send our own people on expeditions, and we also contract with others to procure plant specimens from all over the world. In each case we have to make sure the identity is correct. Then the National Institute of Health, which funds our cancer collections, contracts chemists to run them through various tests to see if they might be effective against cancer.

Our program has been in existence for 18 years, but until recently, it took pretty much a shotgun approach. Now we're switching to a rifle technique. We're aiming for what seems to be most promising, omitting less interesting species. As we do this we compile lists and check off what we have and what we don't have. Each day the list of what we have screened grows and what we have left to look at shrinks, so diminishing returns are setting in. And, the cost of research keeps going up, just because the more common and readily accessible things have already been checked off.

For the preliminary screening we don't even get our hopes up, but if the screening goes well, they'll want us to get a lot more material. First they ask for just 3 pounds. But the second time around they want 50 or more. At that time, they look at different systems and try to determine what the active chemicals are. After that, if it still shows promise, and doesn't show any signs of unmanageable toxicity, then they'll start what we call human clinical treatment. All this might take something like ten years. It's a slow process, involving lots of safeguards.

The question of toxicity and herbs is a big one. All plants contain toxins in limited quantities, and a few plants contain large quantities. Those in the latter category are definitely in the minority. Usually, the more a plant is studied, the more toxins are discovered. Pennyroyal, in moderation, is safe, but it can cause death if overdosed. People must become aware of the hazards. A mild thing can be made dangerous by being concentrated. Wintergreen could be as dangerous as pennyroyal. A woman in Colorado took oil of pennyroyal, which was much more potent than the plant as a whole. She died from an overdose. Any oil can be dangerous if it is concentrated and overdone. In a large enough quantity, even water will kill you. To take a personal example, poke is known as a poison but it is sold in herb stores with the implication that it's good medicine. It also happens to be one of my favorite foods. I eat poke leaves but I know how to prepare them by eliminating the toxins through the right cooking procedures.

Another problem arises when people go foraging and don't know what they're doing. One couple mistakenly harvested foxglove for comfrey and drank the tea, with fatal results. People often confuse one herb for another. Baneberry root has been mistakenly gathered for parsley, and its root has been mistaken for horseradish and Jerusalem artichoke. Colchicine, derived from the autumn crocus, is used for gout today as the plant was 2,000 years ago. It's grown here as an ornamental bulb and has sometimes been confused with onions or leeks, and it has killed.

I'm glad to see the increasing use of herbal remedies, but we can't assume that God made everything harmless—there are lots of dangers when people aren't fully informed. The celandine is another example. It is a wildflower, a member of the poppy family, and it has been confused with parsley. Hellebore and henbane are two poisons that are sometimes confused with edibles like chicory. Pokeberries have been picked instead of elderberries, but I don't know of any fatalities. The FDA has a "hit list" of herbs that should not be consumed by novices. Make no mistake about it.

I'm personally experimenting with yohimbe. I would not recommend it to anyone else. I wouldn't even give it a yellow light. It's supposed to lower blood pressure and contains some of the same chemicals as the Madagascar periwinkle. It has a reputation in Africa as an aphrodisiac. I may consume it, without the nurse knowing it, and then we'll check to see if it lowers my blood pressure. I ran it through the cancer screening program.

Today we see much advocacy of herbal medicine, but we rarely get scientific proof. Certainly, a lot of it can be dangerous if you aren't careful. On the other hand, it's a fact that more people are hit by falling airplanes than are poisoned by herbal medicine. I'd say more than 10 percent of the old wives' tales have some truth to them, so they shouldn't just be dogmatically dismissed. Shall we halt the air traffic before we halt the herbal traffic? Remember, in my grandmother's day, herbs were all there was, so they tended to develop a reliability factor back then just by necessity. And my 101-year-old grandmother hadn't heard about the carcinogen safrole in her sassafras tea!

By taking a scientific approach to the domain of herbs, my hope is that people will start to rid themselves of superstition and herbal hearsay. I'm not asking people to be fearful of all herbs, but we do need to look at the evidence. And remember, there's a lot we still don't know.

One of the "old-timers" in the world of natural healing, *Stan Malstrom* has done research in the fields of cancer and physics. After his son was cured of illnesses through natural healing, Malstrom began studying massage therapy and nutritional counseling, and acquired his first degree in natural therapy in 1953. When he first learned natural healing in the early 1950s, he experienced threats and harassments because of his beliefs.

In addition to a master's degree in science from the University of Utah, Malstrom received a naturopathic degree in 1975.

A tall man with a dignified manner, Malstrom says he has seen many changes since the early days. "We were underground and now we're coming out. Some of the books I have on my shelf would have been suppressed years ago."

Stan Malstrom

The more I study, the more I realize there is no physicist, chemist, or anybody in the world who can adequately explain what nature can or cannot do. You can duplicate sea water so completely that you can run the substitute through a technical analysis, and show exactly what's in it—you have it all right there on a graph—it is identical with sea water to the Nth degree. But if you put a fish in the sea water it lives; if you put the same fish in the man-created water it dies. There is a life element there that neither science nor anyone else can measure. This is the thing we are missing in the general science community.

When it comes to looking at herbs from a scientific point of view, this is precisely the element which I think we should consider. In nature there are countless things which we cannot successfully duplicate; I seriously doubt that we will ever be able to. Yet, this does not deny their beneficial properties.

Actually, I came to have an appreciation for herbs only after thoroughly grounding myself in science. Upon returning from World War II in 1946, I took a job with the Atomic Energy Commission. I stayed there for two years, until I was able to return to school to work on a doctorate in administration at the University of Utah. (Originally, I had intended to enroll in a pre-med program because I had always been interested in health care.)

185

Stan Malstrom
Orem, Utah

During my spare hours at the university, I worked with the cancer research program. It turned out to be really distressing work. The research we were doing involved radiating dogs, checking the symptoms, and then finding out all the possible things that could happen to them. I can't tell you how much I detested it. I didn't like hurting the dogs that way. We would see them develop big sores, lose their hair, and then get violently ill. When I look back on it, the whole thing seems both ironic and barbaric. Ostensibly, they were trying to see what they could do to eliminate cancer. But of course they never did, and they are still carrying on the same type of experiments instead of looking into the more positive realms of cancer prevention through exercise, diet, and herbal applications.

Today we have so many factors, including stress and various toxins in the environment, which may lead to cancer. We find tremendously high rates of fallout of hydrochloric acid in industrial areas. Your body just doesn't know how to handle all the things you are constantly breathing in.

For most people, there doesn't seem to be much to do about it. But more and more, we're learning of herbs and clays that can help remove the various toxins—mercury, lead, and so on—out of your body. There are more ways than you might imagine.

Using diatomaceous earth, which comes from the ocean's diatoms, is one way. Sometimes we forget about the medications from the sea. It is said that all told there are more than 200,000 herbs on the earth, and of these, at least 10,000 come from the sea. Many herbs are cleansing elements. They work by putting minerals, vitamins, enzymes, and so forth in balance. That way the body works— in balance; it simply cannot work when it's out of balance.

In any case, my own awareness of the benefits of herbs came at the time when I was still working in that cancer research program, and my son was born. Right from the start, he was in and out of hospitals. For the first two years of his life, he was afflicted with lung and respiratory problems. As long as he kept going to the hospital, things just didn't get any better. Finally, he almost died. At that point, my wife talked me into trying natural methods. It was a desperate move, and, of course, I was very skeptical since I had this heavy medically oriented background. I told her there was no way those old folk remedies could be better than scientific ones, but if she wanted to try them, go ahead.

Well, she started giving our son vitamins and changing his diet—and using these seemingly unusual things like garlic enemas, to clean out his accumulation of penicillin and other prescribed medications. Well, as it turned out, that was the first time he had gotten better without going to the hospital in more than two years. He didn't get sick again for several months. Then, my wife did the same things and he got well right away. By this time, I had to admit that there might be something to all these old-fashioned herbal cures.

Since I was still working on my doctorate, I had access to the library stacks, and I started digging through whatever herbal books were available. I discovered that mullein, lobelia, cayenne, and comfrey had often been successfully used for bronchial infections. Before long, I also found out, by reading some of the old pharmaceuticals, that garlic had been highly regarded throughout the centuries as one of the best blood purifiers known to man. Then I started going further. I became fascinated with such herbs as goldenseal. The more I studied, the more I thought, "Somebody's really missing the boat!"

According to virtually all accounts, up to present times, herbs, it turned out, were viewed as nature's "drugs." No wonder. When used properly, they contain everything the body needs: vitamins, minerals, acids, salts, and more.

In the midst of my herb research, I felt relieved to quit

the cancer program. Instead, I started to work at a place called the Utah Research and Development Company. Basically, my job involved figuring out the physics of missile reentry—what would happen at specific altitudes and densities when missiles reentered our atmosphere.

All the while, natural healing was increasingly becoming a part of my life. If one of my fellow workers had a kink in his neck or a back that was hurting him, I would give him massage therapy. Or if somebody had digestion problems, they would come to me and say, "What do I do for this?" Usually I could make it better. Pretty soon, I had built a modest reputation.

About this time the choice was becoming obvious—either I would continue with science and research or I would go the so-called natural way. So I decided. I quit the research and kept up my massage therapy and nutritional counseling.

Since then, I've learned more and more that the real name of the game is prevention. If you treat your body right, it will take care of you. Herbs won't do much to help the body if you eat sugar, smoke, or drink alcohol. All of these things tend to slow down the active properties of the herbs. There is no way of avoiding it; you have to keep your diet clean and keep away from toxins so the herbs can work faster.

A lot of our kidney problems today are the result of drinking too much soda pop and coffee and sugar. You simply have to eliminate junk foods from your diet to stay healthy. All told, there are 75 miles of "tubes" running through the kidneys which act as debris filters. Nitrates are especially detrimental to the kidneys. If you have kidney problems, beneficial herbs might be marshmallow root, goldenseal, cayenne, cranberries, watermelon seeds, and corn silk. Whatever your health problems might be, it is really important to first clean out the impurities that are clogging your body.

By getting your energy flow going better, you can help your body to heal itself. Eventually, the body will take over and start its own rebuilding. It isn't like taking a shot of penicillin today and getting rid of your infection tomorrow. It is more like putting into your system the required elements for regeneration and then watching them take over.

Nutrition, of course, is extremely important, but be careful in using supplements. Often when people try to "balance themselves out" with vitamin supplements they tend to overdo one area and underdo another. Supplements are only really needed to get yourself out of a hole. They are helpful when your reservoir is empty. Admittedly, sometimes it takes a lot of water to fill a reservoir. But once the reservoir is full, it may take only a trickle to keep it that way. When people get too heavily into megavitamins and other supplements, the system has to work harder just to control them. In some ways, overdoses of vitamins can have the same effects as drugs.

There are actually just a handful of basic herbs which work for a great many of our common problems. If I were going to be stranded on a desert island with no natural vegetation, I'd probably want to take with me cayenne, garlic, lobelia, goldenseal, and echinacea. But these are just the basics; it would depend, for you, on your individual needs. For example, hawthorne berry is probably the best remedy for many heart ailments. It strengthens the tissues of the arteries and stimulates the flow of blood. Comfrey is another excellent body builder and a good cold preventative; it's very helpful for mending broken bones. Hopefully, on that island, I'd be able to find seaweed, such as kelp and dulse, since these two are particulary advantageous for the thyroid.

So many of us today have lost the ability and the knowledge to heal ourselves—certainly that was the situation when my son was born. More than ever before, people have to learn to become responsible for their own bodies. In modern times, we've forgotten how; but no one else is going to do it for us.

Herbs represent just one way of healing. They are not a panacea. To be most effective, they should be combined with exercise, diet, and a positive mental attitude. Fasting is another important factor.

Ever since I've been involved in nutritional counseling—ever since I switched careers, so to speak—I have felt a lot of personal pressure. But now things are changing. When I was first starting, there would only be about 24 or 40 people at a health gathering. But now the convention halls are filled with as many as 6,000. Many of us were underground but now we're coming out. Some of the books I have on my shelf today would have been suppressed years ago. Now there is enough of a grassroots movement, enough government people and their families involved, that it is unlikely we will see the tide reversed.

It is as if the people are regaining an inherent right. If you know how to go into your own backyard and pick dandelions, if you know how your carrots and beets can help you, then you will know how to stay healthy. You won't need to rely on prescription drugs.

As an herbal practitioner in Vancouver, B.C., *Norma Myers* works among government circles to lobby for legislation more favorable to plant people, and she urges other herbalists to share their information. Mainly, she would like people to grow their own herbs and become more educated in healthful living. "It's no use just giving a man back his health," she notes. "You've also got to teach him to use his energies wisely and for the betterment of mankind."

Presently, Myers grows herbs in the mild, Mediterranean-like climate of southern Vancouver Island where her goal is to develop a residential school of herbalism.

Norma Myers

Everywhere you go you see people exercising more, changing their diets, and asking more questions about herbs. It is a universal trend, but that doesn't necessarily mean they know what they need to know. It just means they are trying.

Unfortunately, many of these people are taking both the wrong herbs and too many herbs. Because of this, herbs that used to be common are becoming harder and harder to find. To understand the energies of herbs means to know when to take them and when not to take them, how much to take, and for how long. A key philosophy in herbalism is being missed.

We find that many who are interested in herbs turn out to be among the worst conservationists. They are literally destroying many herbs by picking them, drying them, and storing them on a shelf where they just sit. By the time a year goes by, most of the energy has left the herbs, and they are thrown out. Then a whole new stock is picked. Many people are storing herbs for years and years when they only need them for a few weeks, or sometimes for just a few days.

After 15 years of observing the plants, I have come to believe that herbs work not so much because of biochemistry and nutrition as because of energy fields. Medicinal

Norma Meyers
Vancouver, B. C., Canada

herbs have powerful energy fields. You can feel the energy when you take them into your body.

I have two beliefs that have grown out of feeling the energies of the herbs. The first is that these plants were made by the same Creator that made you and me. I was not a religious person when I first came into contact with plants. But because of their influence on me I have now become a religious, or spiritual person. The plants have given me an understanding. I try to figure out where they came from and I believe the Creator that made them and made me had a design in mind. Wherever animals or plants or humans live, they were meant to live together as part of a bigger family. Not just the humans alone . . . but humans were meant to live with animals, and with plants, as part of a bigger ecological family. I believe that wherever there are people, animals, or birds, plants were given for that area to keep those animals, birds, and humans in good health.

The other belief that comes out of feeling the plant energies is that when all these ecological factors were created on this earth, God had certain laws for the health of animals, the plants, and the humans. And here I use the term *divine laws*. If people could only live by these divine laws, they could live in health and happiness. Unfortunately, the happiness factor in our human civilization is weak. I feel that people will have to learn once again what these divine laws are. They are not just physical—not just what diet you eat, how much exercise you have, or whether or not you take herbs. Those are not the only divine laws, those are simply the physical divine laws. There are also mental and spiritual laws.

It's no use just giving a man back his health. You've also got to teach him to use his energies wisely and for the betterment of mankind. I like to encourage a sense of conservation among would-be herbalists. To do this, I take people out to the woods to feel the energy of the trees—

the arbutus, the maple, all the different trees. I want them to feel that, because when people get closer to being part of the pattern, then they won't be so destructive.

When people say they want to become herbalists, the very first thing I try to teach them is to keep their herb gathering to a minimum. I try to discourage people from picking immense amounts of wild herbs. Our present civilization has wiped out so many of the fields and woods and turned them into cities and blacktop. There is only a small percentage left, and if everybody gets interested in herbs and goes out and picks bags of them (which they don't need), it will be terribly destructive; they really need only a very, very small amount for health. One thing they can do is to make more alcohol tinctures. Because tinctures can last about 35 years, you don't need nearly so many herbs as are being used now in other ways.

I feel that there are three kinds of herbalists with different responsibilities. First are persons who are family heads. They should have their own herb gardens and try to pick as few wild herbs as possible for the winter. And the herbs they pick should be mostly herbs to *prevent* illness. Everybody seems to be interested in herbs, but they're not doing enough hard work in getting their home gardens going. You can get as many as ten herbs in a very, very small space. Yet when I go through the city here I don't see many herb gardens—only a very, very few. The main herb gardens I see are "left over" from 50 or 60 years ago. I just went past a house today where someone, a long time ago, had planted violets, feverfew, coltsfoot, periwinkle, and lily of the valley, a walnut tree, and some comfrey plants. You don't see such gardens very often today.

In a second category of herbalists are people who are just simple herbalists, who have a general knowledge. These people should pick only the amount of herbs they are going to use. And they shouldn't throw away their herbs when they have finished for the season. They should preserve them for foot baths, hand baths, sitz baths, and so on. In general, people who are into actual herbal practice should be encouraged to pick far fewer herbs, but especially to arrange for the cultivation of herbs on an acre of their own land.

So many of the people who are interested in herbs— both young and old—have to buy them from the stores. I don't think that's right because I don't think it is going to fit into the way civilization is going to go, and I don't think it fits into conservation either. I don't even think it fits into quality. I believe that the quality of herbs that are grown and picked by the home owner and the herbalist are of a far higher quality than herbs that are brought in from other places such as Europe. Farmers in Europe sell on the auction markets. One good company may buy the best of the lot—then the rest of less quality goes to other buyers. Moreover, a lot of the herb material that is brought over here is no longer fresh by the time it gets into the stores. The people who have bought it are not going to throw it away if it's not sold by the end of a year. They're going to keep it and try to sell it the next year. And the next year and the next. I want to see more herbs grown in North America, and more of these grown in home gardens.

There is a third kind of herbalist that we haven't discussed yet. This is not the herbalist who just has knowledge of herbs but rather the herbalist who has been given a special gift by God; he is given the gift of healing, and people are healed by his presence, by his prayers, and by the laying on of hands, by his touch. And when it is needed, he also gives them spiritual instruction, a work for which he has been prepared and trained over a period of many years. This is a very, very special kind of herbalist, one who truly knows the use of herbs. When a person in a North American Indian tribe becomes acquainted with the herbs, he is considered to be chosen by God to take care of his community of people. Over a period of years, he is going to learn not just the herbs but a very great deal about life, so that he can be a good counselor to his people.

There is one other factor in conservation—the distinction between culinary and medicinal herbs. A number of herbal farmers are growing culinary herbs, so that some people think there are many herbal farmers. But I don't feel that is so at all. To really prepare for the future, we are not thinking just of illness prevention, which comes with the culinary herbs, which are good for digestion, good for preventing gas in the stomach, and so forth. We are thinking of medicinal herbs. Real herbalists—the ones with the deep knowledge, the special healers who know both herbs and the healing power of prayer—must have very special medicines because they are not dealing with people who are just trying to maintain health, they are dealing with people who may be dreadfully sick. Medicines for people who are very sick are quite different from the medicines suitable for people who are fairly healthy and who are just eating from the kitchen garden and drinking a few herb teas for their health.

So there should be a mutual concern for the medicine herbs. That's why for the last two years I have been collecting seed. I have gathered what I consider to be the very best types for healing, from my friends who have culinary gardens—and I've gone into the woods to gather the best medicine plants. Of these, I have made a list of about 200 plants that I consider to be medicinal for really ill people and that an herbalist needs to have in his dispensary. Of the 200, about 120 will be growing on farms. Many of them can't be obtained from wholesalers; you won't find them even in Europe. To get them, I have to go deep into the woods.

For example, I'm constantly running out of true, quality Oregon grape. This happens to be one of the best medicines for the liver, and I'm going to need it in the future. To get this grape I have to go to the Chilliwack Mountains. There I have to find an area where the tree planting of a big logging company has been growing for a few years. There are a few spots on Vancouver Island where the trees are getting quite tall now and, because of selective cutting, there is now some openness under the trees, a new undergrowth, and Oregon grape is coming up.

To find these spots and get to them and find the fresh Oregon grape is quite a task, and it takes so much time. If we could only get enough Oregon grape plants growing on farms, it would be a tremendous saving. I can't continue trekking to a place 80 miles away, up a mountain for hours, and come back with what little I do. Why, the next time I go, it may be snowing and maybe I can't get in. I just don't have the time to go that far. And expense is also a factor.

For one plant that I want right now—and there's only a wee bit of it in Victoria—I would have to go 250 miles north, then hire a boat that would cost probably $300 for the round trip. I would have to go up a sound called Knight Inlet, to a bay. After that, I'd have to climb trees, that are extremely hard to climb, to get the plant out of the moss that's growing on those trees. If I couldn't make it until the end of the season, I couldn't go in at all, because winter's really bad in that inlet.

I have the same problem with devil's club. It can only be picked in the winter. It grows in marshes and swamps. I have to wear a raincoat because it is raining—with snow on the ground and water in the ditches. So picture me trying to use a shovel and pitchfork to pull these roots out—my hands are freezing with cold and there is no place to cook my supper. Finally I ask some logger if he will put some potatoes in the oven for me, and then I go back with my cold hands and try to pick more roots.

If we could only have some herb farms in suitable locations, where there are some swamps, the plants are really easy to grow. It is just that nobody has realized that we've got to have medicinals in North America within easy distance of the herbalists. So I would suggest that there be far more herbal farms, herbal cooperatives, and a better marketing system with higher standards. Also, if transportation problems are going to occur in the future, which seems likely, there should be less importation of herbs.

Because of the increased interest in herbs and the change in people's attitudes towards herbalists, herbalists are no longer being ridiculed. It's absolutely amazing. People in all walks of life are discussing these things. Even at social gatherings, they are discussing various methods of health. Well, if more and more people are going to become interested in nutrition and in herbs, there is going to be a very great shortage. I can name herbs that already you just can't get.

If yellow dock goes into short supply, we've got to have people farming yellow dock. But such herbs should be grown by organic and biodynamic farmers. And, they should be mixed, there shouldn't be acres and acres of lily of the valley and acres and acres of yellow dock, but they should be mixed. There should be trees and shrubs and low plants—companion planting. We should grow mixtures of plants that are compatible with one another; one plant can make use of another's shade. You have to pick and choose according to the growth needs, the soil needs of the plants, and companionship needs of the plants. It has to be studied. Which herbs are in short supply? Which herbs are dying out? Which herbs like one another?

One last thing. We need to try to lift up the spiritual values of the whole community, among both the people who are buying and using the herbs and the people who are producing the herbs. I believe that a great deal more has to be done toward raising the general spiritual level of the people on this continent, and that applies to herbalists as well as to the general community.

Herbs provide nutrition and they affect health, and health includes the health of the body, the mind, and the spirit. You can't change physical health for the better without improving the mind and improving the spirit. In treating people, I have discovered that when they put their bodies in shape, their spirits start to shine, and they have a better chance to express the real, true "self" inside. Cranky people become pleasant people. Cranky families become happy families. I see that all the time.

So I feel that our work as herbalists is more than just healing people. If you heal a person one month, the next month he is going to be sick again from some other factor. If you save a person from death by the use of herbs and nutrition, he is still going to die, everybody has to die sometime. People are free to move around, free to undergo stress, free to face problems and challenges. As a result, there will always be variation in these health factors. But the real reason for the healing of people is that, with good nutrition through herbs, you can have better bodies, better minds—and better spirits.

CHAPTER SEVEN

Backcountry Survival

LONG BEFORE MAN learned how to grow crops, he had to know how to find his food and how to distinguish between the healthful plants and the poisonous ones. Plant wisdom made the difference between having a full stomach and malnutrition—and possibly death.

During these ancient times, poisonous plants were often valued as much as healthful ones. In fact, the word *toxic* comes from an expression meaning "arrow poison" and refers to the initial plant applications for use on prey and foe. The Ebers Papyrus, which dates to about 1500 B.C., gives precise information on a wide variety of toxins used in ancient Egypt.

Today, most of us have forgotten or simply grown up ignorant of the foraging knowledge that was once our second nature. Because of this we must use a high degree of caution when we select foods from fields and woods. Such common poisonous plants as oleander, jimson weed, and the leaves of rhubarb plants may be no farther away than the front yard. Nonetheless, when done with the right attitude and understanding, foraging offers rewards that are as practical and nutritious as they are tasty.

203

No longer is foraging simply a matter for the casual hobbyist or the weekend backpacker. With close to one-quarter of the world's population facing chronic malnutrition and hunger, we find ourselves once again confronting some of the basic survival questions of our ancestors. What is growing around us that is fit to eat? And, can we gain our sustenance from these plants? So far, we have barely scratched the surface. Out of an estimated 80,000 plant species that are considered non-poisonous, only about 3,000 are used for food. And more than half of all human food energy and protein comes from just three domesticated grains—wheat, rice, and corn.

For both underdeveloped and developed countries, the practice of foraging can be both economically rewarding and nutritiously sound. So common a "weed" as the dandelion may contain upwards of 5,000 International Units of vitamin A (the RDA—recommended daily allowance) in a mere half cup of the cooked stuff. Or, 100 grams of primrose-willow can supply 12.7 milligrams of iron, versus just 8.8 milligrams for a similar quantity of beef liver.

To get the full food value from wild plants and herbs, the season of picking is important. Leaves and flowers are usually most nutritious when they are picked in the spring and early summer. Berries and seeds, on the other hand, can be easily gathered in the late summer and fall, just before they drop from the parent plant. And roots can be foraged at virtually any time of year, although they are especially nutritious in winter. Foragers and teachers such as *Robert Menzies, Rosemary Gladstar,* and *Reid Worthington* point the way to the wealth of food that awaits picking.

Robert Menzies is a tall, lean man with dark, blazing eyes. He comes from a long line of plant people. Walks in the woods with his grandfather kindled Menzies' obsession with plants and trees. Later, backpacking trips into the mountains taught Menzies the knack of backcountry survival.

A dynamic man who has worn many hats, Menzies is employed as a consultant in the fields of agribusiness and landscape architecture. In 1972, he visited China, where he toured nurseries and greenhouses.

To his peers, Robert Menzies is one of the most knowledgeable and colorful characters among the herbal community. He calls himself a cook, botanist, plant-person activist, romanticist, sentimentalist, and "doctor of the earth."

Robert Menzies
Mill Valley, California

Robert Menzies

Herbs offer one way to raise consciousness. That's the purpose of my gardens—an educational nursery with over 300 species of herbs. I teach my students the practical aspects of herbs—gathering, picking, transplanting, and propagating. You have to be aware of when to pick the plant so you won't hurt it. I teach students to get into nature and talk to the plants. Always talk to them: it's very important. If you pick a plant, make sure you say, "Thank you."

My experience with survival training in the Air Force influenced me a lot, but my main survival learning came later. After I got out of the Air Force, I had a lot to put back together again. I spent five months alone. *Alone,* you know, is hard. First I went up into the Sierras and did a great deal of packing by myself—"regrouping." Then I went into the Trinity Alps. I fished, backpacked, spent time with the Hoopa Indians. Pretty rowdy.

There are few romanticists; there are few sentimentalists; there are fewer naturalists; I'm a "doctor of the earth." You might call my approach "primal medicine" because I come from all the sciences, yet I am not a scientist—a

different kind of scientist, perhaps. Call my science alchemy, the alchemy of nature. I'm totally attuned to nature and that's survival. At one point I didn't even worry
about paying rent. The question was could I get permission to squat on the land? But if you know how to work
with the plants, you are "medicine," and the people will
see that. You will invariably be called into a home.

Survival is becoming a new and different term. Especially since we have to deal with concrete cities, electrical
overhangs, earthquakes that will break power lines and
gas lines—and where are our feet going to be at that time?
It's much different when you're out there on the land.
Survival is a much different thing. There you are in the
balance of the elements. Is that raccoon or bear going to
get your stash? Are you going to be able to get meat or
vegetables to eat? Are you going to have enough growing
time for vegetables? If you drop into the Mount Shasta
area with me, you'll find there are a few things you cannot
grow during wintertime. And if you're isolated in a cabin,
what you've got is pretty limited.

The tools you use in the garden are very important.
We've been using pieces of obsidian to cut and harvest the
herbs. We're learning how to make these things. I tell
students to stick their hands into it, feel it, touch it. I tell
them about what Brysis Buchanan told me—"the three
A's" of herbology. Be *aware* of what's there—touch it, feel
it, see it. Next, *appreciate* it—be reverent. And lastly, *act.*
Not a day goes by without my showing someone a plant
they were never aware of before. I'm not getting paid for
that. I live it. I'm a plant person trying to teach people
about survival. They are learning survival foraging and
how to make their own medicine.

Herbs are one of the basic things when you're out in the
wilderness. I'm trying to teach students the homeopathic
and macrobiotic approach. The word *survival* is "macrobiotic," from the standpoint that you have to deal with

what you have where you are. In old primal medicine, in the pilgrimages, the true healers or magicians could carry only a certain amount of tools with them. They always had to learn a certain amount from where their feet were.

Spirit to me is like blood; it's tribal. It's a fellowship in which you bear your own and bury your own. My grandfather died to pay for what eventually became my education. I got my B.A. and M.A. at the University of the Pacific. But from my hands today I sense his eyes and much of his spirit. I can touch a tree and know that he touched it, and know that men and women before him touched the same tree, that they looked upon it with the same wonder and the same joy that I do. And the "sap" of the same "being" they perceived is still there. It's an element; it's something you think of as you do the sun, the moon, and the stars. You look at the rivers and the creeks and little children—all in that same spirit of reverence. The same when you grow your own little garden and you're out there playing with the ladybugs! You have a lot to think about. It is all a different school than people know from books. How do you prune a holly? Why does the dogwood flower look like the cross of Christ? How do you climb an apple tree and eat an apple so that bears don't eat it before you?

What I'm talking about is found in 200-year-old books that are still handwritten, books which just don't deteriorate because they're not made out of synthetics—the inks don't fade. They've got recipes for foods with all the different nutrients and even preservatives, which are made up of things like garlic, coriander, and cumin.

I learned a lot from my grandad and my grandma. My grandad used to take me for walks. There are a lot of Menzies who are into the land, but then we came from the land too. That was about the way the rules were. If my grandad had his way, he would have been working all the time; he would have been working on the land. He did work the land, but he had to work in the cities to be able to work on the land. And we all know about that.

To a certain degree my grandad was into the medicinal uses of plants. He wasn't into compounding—but he was certainly into the wines and brews and the land. My grandma was more into medicinal uses, as grandmothers and mothers often are. She did a lot of compounding, which wasn't so much in accordance with any great standardized formula of this or that particular doctor; it was just tried and true. She was very aware of the herbs that she put into the wines, and how to make vinegars with a medicinal effect. This was part of our daily nutrition, the use of garlic, onion, fresh greens, rhubarb (as a laxative), how to build up the soil . . . now that's medicine.

I can't describe the love that comes when a grandfather walks his grandson on the mountain and teaches him about the trees and tries to teach him about the spirit. My grandfather would have loved to dedicate himself, as did John Muir, to walking throughout all the mountains. And he did, as best he could. He looked for plants and he tried to look for the names. The same name that I hold, R. H. Menzies, is assigned to the largest Madrone tree in the world. My grandfather discovered it in Ettersburg, Humboldt County, California.

My people are not botanists. My people are horticulturists and conservationists. My father is one of the directors of the Save the Redwoods League. He's not concerned about having his name known, because he's more rewarded in just knowing that he's personally responsible for saving millions of acres of trees so that our descendants, our kids and grandkids beyond us, will live to see them. My ancestors were people who helped the earth very quietly. I'm the one with the big mouth! I'm told I don't need to be so. True. But I'm trying to help people. I feel that I'm a "nurse" helping to care for Mother Earth.

I remember when I was a little kid, I would sit in a cabin

next to a fire while poetry by Keats, Tennyson, Whitman, or Burns was read to me, poems about the bonny glades, the high heavens, and the grasses that blow away. And I have studied on through graduate programs, but I get tired of my book-learning friends—the people pushing paper in business—when they could all be out in the fields. Here, I'm working with people who are actually using information. They are the only people I care to work with at this moment. I like teaching doctors and nurses because I know they can go out and teach others. I take herbalists up in the mountains; these are the people who are doing the practical work. In the summers, I may take a group of about 80 YMCA kids out on herb walks. I cook for all of them and their counselors. If one of the kids hurts a finger, I have him stick it into pine pitch. It's the best natural bandage. Let the kids see it happen. It's the best way to learn.

People are always making demands on my time, but if it's for Mother Earth, I've got the time. I know I'm very dispensable; all of us are. We're fragile, like seeds in the wind, with a bit of light called intelligence. Renaissance is light at a time when the world can no longer take the abuse. In a time of darkness, there has to be light. I look at it as the Tarot card of the star, or a sleeping city that has a dream state above it, a beautiful vision of light casting rainbow colors or frequencies upon a sleeping city. This is what a renaissance is: a redefining, with the grossness eliminated, and the beauty and subtleness of nature prevailing. It is a time of great frustration and a time of creativity. It is a time of incredible beauty.

Start using plants; they are the source of our renaissance and they will give us strength.

At a very early age, *Rosemary Gladstar* was instructed in the ways of plants by her Armenian grandmother. Upon graduation from high school, she journeyed to the Canadian Rockies and the Trinity Alps in Northern California, where she foraged for herbs. Living close to the earth taught her to respect the miracles of nature.

A petite young woman with a gentle voice and kindly smile, Gladstar more recently has been the driving force behind some of California's popular herbal retreats. Through her organizational efforts, Gladstar and her peers have helped set the course for today's herb renaissance. In addition to the retreats, Gladstar runs an herb store in Guerneville and oversees the California School of Herbal Studies.

Rosemary Gladstar

For several years, from the time I graduated from high school until I came back to Sonoma County to settle down, I never lived in a house that had electricity or running water. I always lived in cabins or camped out, and I just ate the food that grew around me. I may have been foolish, but I learned a lot.

It wasn't the living alone part that was so rough. I love living alone. What made it so rough was the foolish way I went about it—going hiking in the mountains, in the snow, without proper equipment and without proper knowledge. Oh, yes, I came very close to dying. I left my son, Jason, with friends—he was just an infant then—and headed out on a 50-mile hike in the Bugaboo Mountains in the fall. When I started out, it was gorgeous. It was just beautiful. But then I ran into a tremendous snowstorm, and I didn't have anything that I really needed with me. Nothing. I had hardly any food with me—just a head of red cabbage and a handful of raisins. And, of course, as soon as the snow hit, I couldn't just stop and eat along the way. Eventually, I was slogging through about four feet of snow and each step was an immense struggle.

I headed for a small cabin that I knew about, and finally I made it. But I was completely soaked. I was just totally, soaking wet. My matches, which I hadn't rainproofed,

Rosemary Gladstar
Guerneville, California

were completely wet and there was nothing I could do. All I could think of was that there was a famous ski resort about five or six miles farther up. So, I mustered my strength and went on.

When I got there I found that it was off-season, but I found the caretaker. He took me in and I stayed there for about four or five days, just convalescing. I was really very, very sick. As soon as I got better, he snowmobiled me back the 50 miles down the mountain. He didn't let me off easily, either. It wasn't so much what he said, but I got the message really strong. He thought what I had done was a dumb thing. It definitely wasn't a gentle experience. Anytime you do something like that—being totally isolated from everyone else—you learn a lot. And basically, I learned to be respectful of what the planet has to teach you. I learned to give each moment all I have.

Foraging requires more than courage; it requires humility and respect for the teachings of Mother Nature. Herbology is more than learning formulas and chemical constituents. You have to learn to live on this earth with total respect. For most of us, the Indians' way of teaching their young respect for the planet is just plain lacking. We log foolishly, we use electricity foolishly, we collect herbs foolishly. As a result, we grow up with no real knowledge about basic survival. Maybe our grandparents knew it, but we grow up apart from them, so we don't even learn it that way. I guess I was lucky in that sense.

My grandmother came to this country from Armenia, and she brought with her all of the Old World ways. My mother, too, is very Armenian, and she still carries that tradition with her. My family came to this country during a Turkish invasion, so they came very poor, and they really had to know how to survive. As kids, growing up on a farm, we knew from the time we were very young how to go out and gather watercress from the streams or pick miner's lettuce and chickweed from the fields. I didn't learn these plants for knowledge; I learned them as a way of life. We had five kids in our family, and I think the only one who was ever taken to a hospital was my sister when she fell off a horse and broke her leg. If I stepped on a nail or a pitchfork, my parents just naturally knew what to do. In elementary school, when I would do class projects, it was always on plant identification. I still have the notebooks that I did at camp in the seventh and eighth grades.

In lots of ways, I was well prepared for living in the backwoods. So after I graduated from high school, I had enough confidence to just sort of take off. First, I headed for the Pacific Northwest, which, to my way of thinking, is the land of the cold winds of truth. And wherever I went, fortunately, there would always be somebody wiser than myself. Maybe they wouldn't be called herbalists, but they would just know about these things. There aren't many people who live up in the Olympics or up in the Canadian Rockies, so whoever is there, is just like your family. One winter, Jason and I lived 500 miles out in the Canadian Rockies all by ourselves in a turn-of-the-century log cabin. I chinked it and put in all the clay and straw myself.

And another time, after I had come back to Sonoma County from Canada, I got this urge to ride into the mountains on horseback. Actually, I had had this desire since I was very little. When I was growing up on the farm, there was a slaughterhouse not far away where they killed horses and turned them into glue. I used to go there and cry all the time. I really did. So I had this dream of going over there sometime and setting all those horses free. But one, I'd keep and ride off over the mountains . . . out over the Sonoma Mountains. Sure it was a dream of the last cowgirl, a dream which so many people have of riding off into the world. But I have this thing about dreams—you dream them so they can come true.

The only thing different about what actually happened

is that I didn't get my horses from the glue factory. I bought three beautiful palomino horses, one for each of us. By that time, Jason was two years old. Also, a young girl who was 18 went with us. She had never ridden before except in riding rinks in Los Angeles. Jason was strapped to the back of a horse. The only food we took with us was dried fruit, a bag of nuts and raisins; we had no food for the horses either. We didn't take the Pacific Crest Trail, like I'd planned. Instead, we rode various trails up into the Trinity Alps, also in Northern California. It was a tremendously wonderful journey. For four and a half months, we rode every day. Every day we got up about dawn. We would ride until the afternoon, and then we'd pull over to some lake or some valley, or meadow and just relax for a while. We boarded the horses down and rested for the night. And the next day, we got up and rode on. We soon relied solely on the food that we found for ourselves and for our horses. I always look back at that time as a time of immense freedom.

Yet, when I got back I also knew it was time to get to work. I was about 22 by then, and I decided to invite a few friends over to teach them what I had learned from all these experiences. So we started in my living room, in my old house, with four or five students. By the second week there were ten or twelve. Before long there were too many students to fit into my house. So then I started renting buildings, and the program just kept growing. Eventually, it evolved into my herb store, the retreats, and the California School of Herbal Studies.

Today, I must admit that I see myself as a businesswoman and I love it. I simply accepted the responsibility for something that needed to be done. The retreats started out so simply. About nine years ago I asked a friend who lived on a ranch in Occidental if we could have a retreat. We were mainly interested in yoga and meditation, but I asked four herbalist friends to talk to the group.

All told, there were about 24 of us sharing with each other. Now attendance at the retreats ranges from 200 to 500 people, and we meet as often as six times a year.

Even so, with the school and the retreat today, it's just like a big family. The people are so honest and unassuming. I have watched this circle grow for many years, and somehow it just keeps expanding. Maybe the younger herbalists seem naive, but among them you will someday find great teachers and masters of herbal knowledge. Just imagine the knowledge they will have 40 years from now, growing from the dedication and understanding they have today.

The essence and energy of plants goes far beyond my understanding. It goes far beyond scientific understanding. By going out and being with the plants, more than anything else, you gain an intuitive wisdom—the result of working with the plants.

The earlier life I lived, the gathering and foraging, was a hard life, but it was really wonderful. I live a much softer life now. It's softer and busier. In some ways, I've gotten a little spoiled. But no matter what, I know I'll never forget those lessons.

Reid Worthington foraged alone in the mountains, became one of the original members of the Oak Valley Herb Farm, and practiced with herbal remedies for six years in the small Sierra community of North San Juan, California.

Speaking reverently about his commitment to nature, Worthington says his sojourn in the woods taught him to observe and recognize the qualities of plants. "Learn directly from the plants," he says quietly. "Go out and live in the woods for six months. The plants will teach you."

Because of his careful observations of nature, Worthington has been able to provide valuable advice to some of the country's leading herb industries, such as Celestial Seasonings and Universal Tea. By examining a product, Worthington can tell whether a crop has been harvested at the right time, how well it's been dried, and whether or not it's been in any way adulterated.

But his true vocation and love is being in the quiet places in the wild where he can "listen caringly," observe, and learn.

Reid Worthington
Portland, Oregon

Reid Worthington

Herbalists tend to lead a somewhat mysterious existence; the very nature of their profession requires them to make solitary observations. As an herbalist, you can't really afford to be distracted by other aspects of life. Traditionally, herbalists have lived way out on the outskirts of town, where people would rarely see them. Although this may seem secretive, it's very, very practical; it's closer to the woodlands and fields—closer to the plants. Learning directly from the plants is one of the best ways to develop your craft. Go out and live in the woods for six months. Pretty soon, you'll start to see and feel more than you ever imagined possible. And sometimes, magical things happen! When I was living in an isolated cabin in the Sierras, I used to hear at night beautiful choruses of voices singing. It was the most beautiful music I have ever heard. You might call it a mystery; it was the river and the wind singing.

For five years, from 1971 to 1976, I did nothing else but pursue herbs. That was long before I arrived in Boulder to become Celestial Seasoning's chief herbalist and tea taster or before I arrived at my present position designing botanical health and beauty care products. Actually, time spent in the woods ties in with the topic of how large tea manufacturers can determine quality herbs. To find out what

221

the best possible quality is, you have to spend time where the best quality is produced and that's with nature. If you've gathered your own herbs, you're going to know what this means.

Originally, the whole herb trade grew up around individuals in small villages who would supply botanicals to a very few people. Usually these people would have large gardens and they would also go out and gather wild herbs at just the right time; they would handle them properly and dry them in special sheds. Although we're talking about 200 years ago, when it comes to quality, things haven't changed that much. Because herbs lend themselves to small-scale industry, large herb companies must be particularly careful in their dealings.

In San Juan, I worked in the traditional way, and the skills that I learned are the same ones which I apply to my work today. My respect for nature hasn't changed. If I thought there was a danger that I might lose my appreciation of nature's gifts, I'd walk out the door in a minute.

During the whole time I lived in San Juan, I had a routine. It would start in the early spring with the gathering of roots, and end in the fall, again with the roots. In between came the gathering of the leaves and flowers.

During the wet and misty part of spring, I would collect roots of yellow dock and bring them home. I would clean and slice them into thin pieces, and set them by the wood stove to dry. Later, when the weather warmed, and the leaves opened up, my daily routine changed. I'd start the day by working barefoot in the garden. It was a large garden where I would domesticate and study native plants by transplanting them from the wild, and cultivate comfrey, catnip, mints, and many other herbs. After I had worked in the garden for a while, I would take my gunnysack and walk through the hills gathering herbs. I would bring them home, tie them in bundles, and hang them from the ceiling to dry. All through the spring and summer the ceilings in every room were completely covered with herbs. As they dried, I would take them down, gently strip the leaves from the stems, and store them very carefully. Right away, I'd replace the spot in my ceiling with fresh herbs.

At one point, I made a list of the herbs I was collecting, and I came up with a total of 36 that I was gathering in small commercial quantities to sell to suppliers in the San Francisco area. By doing this, I quickly learned how to spot the differences between good and bad herbs. In fact, this is really where I learned the basics of how to test for herb quality.

In the winter, when all the gathering was over, I read herbals and did lots of experiments. I set up a little distilling apparatus, and I would sit in the kitchen all day long extracting the essential oils of the herbs and writing down my observations.

Today, when I do my work, I still keep files of different herb descriptions. It's the same practice that I started years ago; it has just expanded. In evaluating herbs for a company, I start by making notations of the physical appearance. When the herb is delivered, I have to find out if the leaves are whole or broken into pieces. Is there any other material mixed in with the leaves? Next, I check the color. Is the leaf good, vibrant green, or is it turning brown? A brown color may indicate poor drying or storage conditions. I keep notes on all these variables.

After that, I move on to the fragrance or aroma. You'll find that it becomes a very interesting practice when you sit down and try to characterize the particular fragrance of an herb. For example, to my own frame of mind, passion flower has an earthy aroma, something like damp earth, whereas red clover reminds me of sweet hay. It's a beautiful scent, almost like a field in springtime after a rain. And then comes the taste. Some really wonderful herbs have very unusual flavors when you get right down to it. For example, I think of elder flower tea as having a flavor like water you drink from a garden hose on a hot day. It's almost a rubbery flavor, but quite nice just the same.

Ultimately, in the commercial testing of herbs, you weigh all these factors to determine quality. But, interestingly, all of these tests and skills can best be learned by doing your own gathering and preparation. For example, the way you know about whole leaves is if you've gathered a plant and dried it and then stored it carefully. That way you'll automatically know it's best to keep herbs whole until just before you use them, if you want to retain the vital properties. But, of course, on an industrial level, we're talking about compressed bales of leaves that may weigh as much as 200 pounds. They're going to have to be mechanically reduced by a mill. So, you check to see how the herb particles are sifted, since the method of sifting is going to determine the finished quality of the herb. Poorly milled herbs will have a tremendous amount of dust and fine particles. The next time you're in an herb store, pick up a jar and check to see what the pieces look like. If there's no dust, and the herbs look clean, and their color is vibrant, then you're looking at a well-prepared herb.

Today we see an industry which has grown virtually overnight from a specialized craft to a gigantic business. If a person can study with an herbalist and gather herbs, on his own, he will learn quickly. Becoming a true herbalist requires a special dedication, love, and years of study. Proceed slowly and very carefully. Start out with a trust in the plants. Never assume that just because a certain application is written up in a book it's safe to use the herb in that way. Learn by experience.

When I first moved to North San Juan, people started coming to me mainly out of curiosity. They had watched me head into the mountains with my gunnysack and wondered what I was doing. Almost everyone in the community had an interest in nature and its workings. In a sense, they were willing to be guinea pigs for herbal treatments because they wanted to know how they could treat themselves with natural products. One day, not long after I arrived there, a woman asked me for help with an extreme case of sunburn. I prepared two buckets of strong comfrey leaf water, and the remedy worked. So pretty soon people started asking me about other treatments.

I remember walking miles and miles to my neighbor's cabins to deliver herbs. Typically, if somebody had the flu, I'd make up a broth of herbs like plaintain, clever's grass, and yellow dock. I'd strain off the tea, put it in a Mason jar, slip it into my backpack, and head out the door. It was like delivering chicken soup, only it would be the herb broth instead! After people took it, they would usually start to feel their stomachs settle down and pretty soon the fever would dissipate. Generally speaking, the various herb treatments worked really well for common complaints—things like poison oak, sunburns, cramps, and asthma—but for staph infections, which were very common in rural parts of California, I could never seem to find anything to take the place of antibiotics. It wasn't until I had left San Juan that I discovered the antimicrobial properties of the essential oil of chamomile.

There is a need for qualified information in this field. Many people have lost contact with the soil, have forgotten how to gather, dry, and prepare their own herbs. Now, people are discovering herbs for the first time on supermarket shelves. The main thing about being in close contact with nature is that it automatically brings you to a point of close observation, something that is absolutely required to understand nature. If you approach herbs with the right mind and heart, and stay on a good footing, you will find that nature reveals many secrets for understanding the relatedness of all things. There are things that are given to the heart and the eyes when you're out alone in the woods, things that can't be put into words.

CHAPTER EIGHT

Herbal Practices

ALTHOUGH MEDICINAL HERBS can easily be acquired either straight from the field or by purchasing them in a health food or specialty shop, the actual practice of herbal medicine is, with rare exception, restricted to licensed allopathic physicians. The various state laws that contain such provisions are primarily designed to protect us from the kinds of medical quackery that flourished throughout the late nineteenth and early twentieth centuries. But today, when these restrictions are allowed to remain unmodified, they present us with a medical system that is not only prohibitively expensive, but one which effectively discourages most forms of natural healing practice.

Individuals who teach herbalism, own shops, or market herbal products can provide nutritional information and tell how a certain herb will reputedly affect the body in a particular circumstance, but they are strictly forbidden from actually diagnosing or treating an illness. The distinction here is between health treatment, which requires a license, and health education, which does not. Those who do not recognize this distinction must be prepared to face the consequences.

On the other side of the coin, medical doctors can diagnose ailments and prescribe herbs, but as a rule, they receive no meaningful instruction in herbology. It's a Catch-
22 and, ultimately, it is the patient who wants herbal
treatment who is caught.

The situation is further complicated for doctors (and for
individuals who may wish to heal themselves) by the
difficulties involved in procuring medicinal herbs. With
the advent of chemical medicine, particularly in the twentieth century, almost all of the traditional herbal remedies
simply disappeared from the druggists' shelves. Today
only a handful of crude plant substances are listed in all
the catalogs of the major drug companies. The rest have
been superseded by their alkaloid or glycoside derivatives
or else by synthetic drugs. Because of this, even M.D.s
who wish to prescribe herbal treatments are greatly dis-
couraged from doing so.

Some herbs, of course, may be purchased from herb
stores, but these are greatly limited compared with the
total range of medicinal herbs. Generally, herbs that may
be found in stores include only those the FDA has deemed
suitable for labeling and marketing and, accordingly, pro-
claimed as "Generally Recognized as Safe." Granted,
some herbs can be exempted from such listing, but they
must have a long history of use for culinary purposes.
Here one finds the common spices such as basil, oregano,
and parsley.

Any herb that does not meet the requirements for either
the GRAS list or the culinary exemption must be subjected
to thorough testing if a medicinal claim is made. Such
herbs can conceivably be marketed, but if the label indicates medicinal benefits for the herb, the company marketing it is required to prove the safety and effectiveness of
the herb or face FDA misbranding charges. Once a medicinal claim is made, the FDA considers the herb a drug
rather than a food.

No doubt this would be reasonable were it not that to qualify as a "new drug," an herb must be subjected to tests costing between $3 and $5 million and taking from three to five years to complete. These tests are so expensive because the FDA requires that each active ingredient be tested individually against a specific symptom. Herbalists generally contend that these tests don't make sense because of their prohibitive costs and the fact that the very reason a certain herb may prove useful is precisely that its *combined* ingredients, not merely its isolated properties, are effective.

If a way can be seen out of this medical paradox, perhaps someday we will find it in a system that permits and encourages herbalists to work hand in hand with conventional medical doctors. As noted earlier, the models are already available in other customs and cultures.

John Christopher, N.D., *Jeffry Anderson*, M.D., and *Nan Koehler*, a practicing midwife, show us a path which, despite the obstacles, provides a much-needed prescription. Perhaps their way is not perfect—there is, in fact, no such perfection in medicine—but it does offer a time-honored and timely restorative for our present medical woes.

Many herbalists regard the late *John Christopher* as the pioneer of today's herb renaissance. Before he was 34, Christopher was plagued with rheumatoid arthritis, heart ailments, and high blood pressure. These illnesses literally forced him into the study of herbs and a dairy-free diet, to both of which he attributed his recovery.

In his role as herbal trailblazer, Christopher sustained many hardships, both legal and financial. He was arrested five times on charges relating to practicing medicine without a license, and although usually exonerated, he had to pay enormous attorney bills. Up until the time of his recent death, Christopher lectured almost nonstop throughout the United States and in many foreign countries.

One of his last "testaments" appears on the following pages.

John Christopher

For the 35 years I have been in this program I have had to fight most of the time, teaching as a lone wolf, because not many people believed as I did. When I was in my 30s I was teaching something that was practically unknown—people had almost forgotten about herbs. They had gone the doctors' way and were quite thrilled with shots, inoculations, and inorganic drugs; they had pulled away from herbs to a point that very, very few people knew what herbs could do.

Today, the pendulum is swinging our way. We are now in a better condition as far as herbs are concerned than at any other time in the 35 years that I've been involved. More and more, people have begun to get a feel for herbs. The great "universal mind" has picked it up, and people in various places have started the herb program rolling again. I feel rewarded because this has been my life work. I was led to it through my own ailments, and over the years I have come to a point where I can help others.

I'm very pleased with what's going on with herbs today. I have been asked to speak at the National Health Federation conference and to the Cancer Victims and Friends, and to various staffs of M.D.s. It is only recently that herbalists were even acknowledged by these associations. It seems that about ten years ago the interest really started to

John R. Christopher

pick up, and more books have no doubt been written in the last three to five years on herbs than were written in the last 100 years. But not all of the recent books are good. Some of the authors are just borrowing from earlier herbalists. And the same is true even with my herbal remedies. I was almost alone in my formulas for years. But there are thousands now, and many of mine have been appearing with others' names on them. I always recommend that people go back to the pioneers. We are the ones who have been in and out of the courts, in jail, and fighting all these years.

I've been arrested four or five times, but I am blessed in that I always bounce back and roll with the punches. I've been arrested more times in Utah than in any other state. I won all the cases except one. In that incident, a law was passed in 1970 stating that anyone who was examining another individual in any way was practicing medicine. So I was arrested for this on a felony charge and was placed on probation for 18 months. It seems ironic; our forefathers passed a law for the 13 original colonies stating that herbalists should be allowed to practice natural medicine and not be harassed, but there isn't one state in the Union that will give a license today to an herbalist. England, Switzerland, Germany, and India are much more advanced in their use of herbs. Here, herbalists must fight so much.

If it hadn't been that I was more or less forced into a study of herbs, I don't know what would have happened to my own career. I was born with rheumatoid arthritis and later in life was confined to a wheelchair for nine months and sometimes as long as two years at a time. Because I was on crutches so much, I developed high blood pressure and heart trouble. In addition, I had stomach ulcers and many things. I spent six months in a wheelchair with rheumatic fever. But the orthodox doctors were unable to give me any help. They gave me temporary help but then I would get worse again. So I was reading the scriptures and found a number of places where it said to use herbs, and that's what really got me started. For example, in Ezekiel 47 it says, "And the fruit of the tree shall be for meat and the leaf thereof for medicine." And in Psalms, it tells us in words to this effect: "and the grass is for the cattle but the herb is for the purpose of man to bring forth food from the earth." When I read these scriptures along with many others, I realized that the food of the earth is in the form of the herb; that's its purpose on earth. So I began to pick up herbalism through my own investigation.

When I was a teenager, my mother was very sick, suffering from diabetes and dropsy. Many doctors treated her, but one day she told me that a doctor would be coming to the house who would be different from the rest. He came and used iridology to read my mother's eyes and then prescribed some herbs for her. He really awakened my interest. But he later went to jail for his practices, and we weren't able to follow through on the herbs he recommended.

As far as my own experimentation with herbs is concerned, it really began when I was in my upper 20s. My first booklet on herbs was written before I was 30. Young as I was, I had not really embarked on the technical side.

The first teachings I received were from Minnie Allen Raymond. She was a little lady from the East, a natural nurse, and she got me started on the use of carrot juice and other nutrients. She helped me get my health back, and by the time I was in my early 30s, my health was so restored that I could attend Dominion Herbal College in British Columbia. I went back and forth from Fort Lewis, Washington, taking some courses at Dominion; the rest I did as correspondence. Dr. Knowle at Dominion was one of the greatest teachers of all times. He was a very humane individual who loved his students. His main desire, and my desire has been since, to help other people learn what he was teaching.

In the '40s, I went to Tacoma, Washington, where I had my first lessons in zonal therapy from an old German doctor. Then I enrolled in the School of Drugless Therapy in Iowa, receiving my naturopathic degree before going on to Los Angeles to study herbal chemistry with Dr. Shook at the Los Angeles Herbal Institute.

After my training period, I started out with small practices in the late '40s in Vancouver; Olympia, Washington; and Evanston, Wyoming. When I moved to Salt Lake City, they would not accept any more naturopathic physicians, so I practiced as an herbalist. There were no laws against practicing as an herbalist then, no laws for or against, and my practice grew rapidly. In no time at all, I was seeing between 85 and 90 patients a day, with a staff of 14, including masseurs, zonal therapists, and a chiropractor. But my success soon aroused considerable notoriety, which in turn evoked resentment among the professionals in the city. When the opposition seemed to turn to persecution, I was forced to abandon my practice in Salt Lake City and move to a smaller community. By so doing I hoped to continue helping people by keeping my practice on a low-key profile. Sadly enough, I became the victim of newly contrived legislation and I was forced to stop my practice altogether.

What appeared to be a tragic ending, however, turned into a blessed beginning as I stepped into the lecture circuit. Now I visit some 50 cities a year where I talk to thousands of people about my experiences. In fact, my work has gotten so big that I'm in 120 major lecture cities each year. I've been invited to speak in Europe, Asia, India, and Australia. Usually, I'm booked a year in advance.

People should understand, however, that I am not a botanist; I'm an herbalist. A person who has an open mind can do great things with herbs. I don't think even Jethro

Kloss knew the chemical aspects. The Thomsonian program didn't incorporate the technical part. Some of our foremost herbalists never knew the technicalities, the breakdown of the mineral content of herbs. But they knew which herb would aid in healing a certain illness.

Above all, herbs work because the human body has in it all the minerals and substances that are in our Mother— our Mother Earth. But to get the minerals from the earth we have one big problem; that's assimilation. We can go out into a parking lot and get a shovelful of the dust of the earth and put it on a separator, and it will separate the various types of minerals into segregated piles. We can then take each pile and pharmaceutically grind it down to a point of medicinal fineness and put it into capsules and take it. All right, we're getting these minerals: the iron, sulphur, magnesium, and various types of minerals. They are accepted into the body and accepted very easily, but not much of it is assimilated.

The essential thing is that each herb that grows on the face of this earth has its own way of demanding the minerals that it needs. For example, garlic demands sulphur, and it will draw sulphur from the earth. This sulphur, of course, is very beneficial to mankind. The sulphur minerals that are in the earth can be beneficial, but they leave side effects, whereas, the sulphur that has accumulated in the garlic is beneficial with no side effects and no after effects. It is already "assimilated," so it is acceptable to the body.

When we break down the herbs, we find that we lose a great deal of value. With wheat, when we take off the bran and remove the oils, all we have left is the white flour. It is the same way with herbs. For example, if we use the whole herb as a tea, we know that we're not losing anything. But if we make a tincture and certain particles are drawn out, we get only part of the strength of the herb. In tea, the water can draw the healing values and the food values from the herb itself. It seems to be one of the fastest and most complete ways to get the value out of the herb and into the body.

There are different ways of working with herbs, but I have preferred using the herb as food and supplying the body with an abundance of the specific type of herb it needs. It is impossible to find any one herb that will do everything. For example, the urinary system sometimes doesn't function well and we have to have a diuretic. Well, a diuretic will not rebuild a nervous system, just as the nervine herbs will not rebuild the uretheral track. So it is with a bowel that's in a badly polluted condition. We'll give it the food herbs to get the peristaltic muscles and the liver and the gallbladder working properly.

When I first started to use the various herb combinations for bowel problems, I found that some of the herbs would cause so much discomfort that I had to keep changing them around. It took about 12 years before my lower bowel formula was to the point where it would do the job that it's doing now. Over that period of time I would change it in various ways. I would find one herb that would stir up the liver and the gallbladder to a point where the bile would flow out and be mixed with the old fecal matter, but sulphur from eggs and one thing or another would cause reactions and there would be a lot of gas. So we added herbs that would take care of the gas. Then where there was griping, we added other herbs to take care of that. It took a lot of time.

Not all of our combinations, however, have required as much time and experimentation. Some of them come to us in a flash, very quickly, completely outlined. We just jot them down. Once in a while the "universal mind" will drop us a formula in the "snap of a finger." It's all complete in your mind and it's correct. I never have to change those. A number of others have come through experimentation and through prayer. I have been helped by the Lord.

What I've found in my studies is that there are no incurable diseases, but there are incurable patients. Some patients enjoy ill health and can't be healed. They're hypochondriacs. Attitude is a very important part of healing. There's an hour to be born and an hour to die, but with a healthy body and a healthy mind you won't get diseases.

Not until my mid-30s did I begin to feel any good health at all. Before that, I was just fighting to keep alive. Even when I started my practice as a naturopathic physician I wasn't yet quite well, but I was so anxious to open up my office that I didn't take the time out to get completely well. I had just gone on and on and on and never taken time off. So I was just healing a little as I went along but never completely. I sometimes felt that I should stop for a week, or two weeks, or a month and rest—and get myself in good condition. But then I would think, yes, but there are people who want to learn. I just had to keep going.

We hope to build several health spas where we can also have a school. But most of all, we want to have a place where students can learn about herbs in the right way. It is terribly discouraging when a student does not study thoroughly and then goes out and says, "Well, I learned under Dr. Christopher." That's no compliment and it doesn't help anyone. That's why we would like to develop a school and a clinic together so students can learn step by step. The Lord was kind enough to show me the way, and I just want to show the way to others.

Nan Koehler, a midwife and mother of four, specializes in herbs for pregnant women. A sprightly woman whose hobbies include bird-watching and dulcimer playing, Koehler has a master's degree in botany. It was birthing her own children that really sparked her interest in herbal usage.

Koehler began by assisting Jeanne Rose with her herb classes and eventually wound up teaching. Presently, she works with her husband, Donald A. Solomon, M.D., an obstetrician, at their Rainbow's End Farm clinic in Northern California. Their cooperative practice serves as a model for the merging of conventional and alternative medical practices. By consulting each other about particular ailments, questions or concerns, they provide their patients with aspects of both worlds.

Nan Koehler
Sebastapol, California

Nan Koehler

When I was pregnant with my second child, I wanted my first child to see the birth of his sibling. Back then, in 1970, you couldn't do that in a hospital, at least I didn't know of any hospital that allowed that sort of thing. About that time, we were living in Haight-Ashbury in San Francisco, and in a way, we were involved in that whole scene. But I must admit I felt pretty tangential to it because I wasn't really into drugs. Mainly, I was involved in alternative education—A. S. Neal and Summerhill and all. I was teaching at a school, and one of the women I worked with had a baby by herself at home. And nothing had happened—the sky didn't fall, and the baby was fine. That convinced me. I thought, if she can do it, so can I.

To prepare myself, I read all sorts of obstetrical texts, midwifery textbooks, herb books—you name it. The herb books were easy for me since I already knew the plants. I had a master's degree in field botany from the University of Chicago and had even started on a doctoral program. The only thing missing was that I'd never used plants medicinally. They don't teach you that part in school.

To find out those things, I started taking classes with Rob Menzies. And it was through Rob that I met Jeanne Rose. It worked out well because I began to assist in her classes with plant identification. I already had lots of experience teaching biology and botany, so I could easily fit into that niche. The main thing I could do, that I have learned from all my training, is that when I go out walking I can generally tell the name of every plant I see. When I was in graduate school, I enjoyed learning the names of plants, and hiking around. At that time, hardly anyone else was doing this sort of thing.

But before I get too far into that I should tell you that I did have my second son at home. It was a wonderful experience and everything was fine. Some friends were there, but I was my own medical attendant. Nobody else knew anything about it as I did so I was responsible. My first son was able to be there for his brother's birth, so he got to see the whole thing. After that, it seems that I was just propelled into a career as a midwife.

About this time, I also learned that Rosemary Gladstar was going to have her first herb retreat right here where the clinic is now, at Rainbow's End Farm. So I came up here and I did an herb walk because many people wanted to know how to identify wild plants.

Back then, Rainbow's End Farm was called Laney's Ranch, after Helen "Laney" Stevens, who wanted to make it into an "Esalen North," with encounter groups, massage, and all of that. So they had weekend retreats, like Rosemary's, right here in two big barns that used to be part of a winery. Actually, they were like meeting rooms, and people could sleep in the barns or outdoors, or wherever they wanted.

I remember how really wonderful it was to be around people who didn't think I was nuts. You could say, "Oh, I like plants too," and they would say, "Wonderful." You weren't an oddball or something. The group support was just fantastic. You had the feeling that someday we were going to validate our concerns. Then we had the dream of having a school, which Rosemary is now conducting. A lot of other people are now trying experiments in higher education.

I remember sitting in the upper barn, where we have our clinic offices now, with Rob, Jeanne Rose, Rosemary, and other people from Berkeley—all talking about what we were doing and what everybody was doing, and how we were going to legitimize it all.

As we were sitting around, someone was talking about Dr. Christopher's liver flush. And I thought, "liver flush!" If it wasn't one thing, it was another. It went on and on; what you were supposed to do that you weren't doing right—like, don't use a washrag, use a loofa and brush your skin. I made a song about it. I thought it was funny and sang it to everybody. It's a joke and you have to more or less know what I'm talking about. Part of it goes like this:

When I wash and scrub myself with loofa and a brush,
I am clean inside and out, I never smoke or cuss.
Swing and turn Rosemary, live and learn Rob Menzies.
Cayenne pepper when I wake up, salads night and
   noon.
I drink comfrey in my juice, and sleep by the light of
   the moon.
When I want to sleep at night I drink valerian tea.
Lemongrass and chamomile, no pep pills for me.

It's a dance song—an old Appalachian Mountain song— and I can't play it as fast as you're supposed to. You're supposed to play it really fast. We had all these ditties that are really teaching, and I used to hum it a lot.

Later the ranch was sold to Dr. Solomon, and the caretaker's wife, Linda, became the secretary in our office. I don't really think of what we have now as a clinic; a clinic, to me, is open to the public, whereas here you phone and make an appointment. Anybody can come in here, but usually they call and make an appointment. It's a regular schedule and a busy one. We see about 10 to 15 people a day plus go to the birthings. Of course, we have other people helping out.

Because I work with my husband, who's a trained obstetrician, I attend many more births than if I were just working by myself. Before Don and I connected, I would probably go to one birth every month or so. But now we stay up all night long once or twice a week. And believe me, that's a lot with four kids. When I met Don, I was doing herb walks at the Holistic Health Institute down in Mill Valley. He had seen my name on brochures and handouts, and he wanted to learn more about herbs. It turned out he was looking for a midwife to work with, and I happened to be looking for a doctor to back me up in my practice. So we just naturally started working together.

Actually, it's very rare to find a specialist who's interested in alternative health care. Don may be the only obstetrician in the United States who's doing this kind of thing. Specialists have had three extra years of medical school and all the indoctrination that goes along with it, so they're very entrenched in their professional viewpoints. It is hard for them to change. You'll find that most of the doctors who are into alternative medicine are general practitioners.

Partly because of our backgrounds, our clinic is really focused on education. When people come to us we try to help them figure out for themselves, as much as possible, what they may need. We have a large library, and we work right along with them, whether it's a treatment or a birthing. We tell people that even if they are going to give birth in a hospital, they should prepare for it as if they were going to do it alone. That way it really motivates them to read the books, learn the words, and understand what's going on.

I really have no idea what our success rate is with gynecological problems, but I do know that very few people call us back with problems. It's really interesting. The women I talk to say the program works really well. We've now published our birth statistics.

When people come in, we'll first talk about their diets and about using herbal teas, as well as simple changes in their lifestyles which might alleviate a particular condition. If that doesn't work, then we go the regular medical route. But we always tell them about the alternatives. For example, if a woman comes in who's experiencing irregular periods, Don might tell her the medical options of handling it, such as birth control pills, giving her a D & C, or maybe performing an endometrial biopsy. Or, if she should wish, she could do the alternative, which might mean getting on an alkaline diet and systematically taking vitamins and herbal teas. The teas we tell them about are usually just classic Dr. Christopher recipes with standard herbs that are used for any kind of menstrual problem. They work really well so, actually, only about 10 percent of our practice involves drugs.

The most common things we have to deal with are yeast infections and trichomonas. With the natural treatment for trichomonas, you have to be really systematic, with treatment every day for around four to six weeks; whereas, with the chemical approach, the problems might disappear in a day. For obvious reasons, most women don't have the patience for that. Some of them will try it sporadically, and then say, "Oh, give me the pills." The problem with just taking pills for trichomonas—and it's the same for yeast infections—is that you won't get lasting effects. That really involves diet changes, taking herbs, and getting more rest. These infections are part of the vaginal flora that are always present, but if your vaginal secretions are either too acid or too alkaline (if the pH factor is off), then the yeast will start growing and you'll get really itchy.

To me, a woman's use of herbs is an external symbol of how well she is taking care of herself. We do home visits with the people who want to have home births—and when I see the woman who has lots of herbs around and uses herb teas regularly, I know right away that she will have an easy birth. There's something about making the teas. To me, it's almost a magical process. In a way, you don't even have to drink the tea, it's just the time you take to do it, and the time you spend thinking about your birth in a positive way. It's a sort of symbol, a flag or affirmation. If a woman will do that, she's probably willing to do everything else that goes into making a good birth.

Of course, certain teas have proven to be highly effective. For example, I advise the pregnant ladies to drink red raspberry leaf tea. This is a traditional herb used by the Indians and many other cultures to prepare the uterus. It's an excellent muscle toner and a good source of minerals, calcium and magnesium. If you take one cup a day throughout most of the pregnancy, with four cups a day for the last three or four weeks, your uterine contractions will be stimulated, and you will go into labor a lot easier. Many women in labor have very violent chills; it is exhausting. But if your body has the proper minerals, you won't have those chills.

And then, of course, let me tell everybody about comfrey. We have comfrey growing all around the farm. It is just excellent, and I like to take it to every birth. I like to have people make and use about three or four pots of comfrey tea each day after their birthing. Also, they should take comfrey sitz baths, because it makes them heal much quicker. Usually women bleed for a long time after a birth, but with comfrey tea they quit bleeding almost immediately. If they stay in bed and drink the comfrey, it just lasts three to five days and they're done with it. Whereas, with standard medical practice it can sometimes take another six weeks.

Lavender is another herb I often take with me, especially if I think the woman is going to have a hard time. When you're under stress, the scent of lavender is wonderfully soothing. There are also specially prepared birthing tinctures you can buy in stores, but I haven't really gotten into those because I like to grow, gather, and make my own.

I tell people about the most common weeds that are all around, those they might see every day, and what they can do with them. A few of the common herbs in people's yards are plantain, malva, sow thistle, dandelion, chickweed, and all of the mints. Of course, there are lots of others depending on where you live.

We always show people how to make teas as simply as possible—actually they're called herbal simples—so any person can make them. We tell everybody, make sure you brew the teas in enamel rather than metal. That is really important. If you want to use the medicinal alkaloids or aromatic oils, you have to prepare the herbs in the proper way or you'll destroy them. So don't let the herbs touch any metal. Don't even stir them with a metal spoon or use a metal strainer or anything like that. If you are interested in the minerals, it doesn't matter. Or, if you just want it as a beverage, it doesn't matter either. But making a tea in a glass jar is really the best way. You can just put the herb in a glass jar, pour some water over it, and sip it throughout the day. That way it gets stronger and stronger as the day goes on.

Of course, some medicinal teas are so bitter that you can't drink them. The inner bark of the white pine is like that, but it's the strongest astringent drink I know of. It can stop mucus flow or a chronic runny nose and bronchitis really well. But, in order to drink it, you'll want to add a little bit of milk to take off that bitter taste. I always tell people to avoid honey, since it alters the taste of the tea and makes the drink acidic.

Even kids can get used to the taste. In fact, I've had a

good success rate with my kids, actually 100 percent. My kids all drink herb teas, so I can easily deal with most ailments that come up. With major things, such as accidents, Don can apply his medical skills to stitch them up. That's really about all he has to do, from a professional point of view, for our children.

What I'm really interested in right now is pediatrics, even more so than midwifery, because in recent years we've gathered a whole body of knowledge about how to have a successful home birth, but there's not much about child rearing and pediatrics. Today, more women are interested in basic nutrition and breastfeeding at home. And the "Dr. Spock" advice books just don't serve them. So I'm increasingly putting energy into making changes in that area and having people learn about home remedies with their children. I've got to admit, one of my fantasies is to go into all the hospitals and smash the nursery windows and let the babies out; just like a suffragette, I can envision it. I think it's terrible the way it is now. A nursery is like a jail. Babies should never be stashed like that. The worst part about hospitals is the way they isolate us from what's happening.

The thing that actually started the seed for my whole change of consciousness was the way things happened when my first husband died. We had been at a meeting together and he left first, on a motorcycle. I came along in my van, behind him by about half an hour or so. On the side of Mount Tamalpais, coming down the mountain, the accident happened. There was the motorcycle in the ditch. I recognized it and stopped. I said, "Oh, that's my husband!" A policeman said, "You'd better get in the car; I'll take you over to the hospital." He was pronounced dead on arrival. But . . . I recalled that the sheriff said he was alive when he came to the scene of the accident.

They didn't tell me much on the way to the hospital. I didn't see his body even at the hospital. Nobody asked me anything. They kind of shunted me off to a side room, and the coroner told me that he was dead.

It turned out that it was a coroner's case; they wanted to see if he was drunk or whatever. He was a chronic asthmatic. I wondered if the ambulance attendant tried to give him oxygen without clearing his airways. He also might have had trouble with asthma on the way, maybe he was driving too fast or something, hit a patch of fog. I don't know. The next day, with our boy, my first son, I went to see what had happened in the accident. But it wasn't "real" to me or to my boy.

They kept his body at the mortuary. You seem to have no control over what they do. I told them I didn't want anything to do with it the way they were handling it. And I didn't want him buried; I wanted him cremated. They had to dress him to have him cremated. I had to bring some clothes, and I told them I wanted to dress him. They wouldn't let me to do that either. I went to look at him. It was such a release for me to see his body and to touch him. It was just wonderful, and I wished I had brought our child. At the time, I was thinking about bringing him, and everybody said, "Don't bring your child. It will be terrible and he'll freak out forever." But as I was driving home I was very upset that I hadn't brought my son to see his dead father. It seemed like such a loss.

After that, I decided that when my second child was born, I would make it okay; my son would be involved. He would see his brother being born. And that's what I did. That's what started the evolution of my herbal education.

Jeffry Anderson, although trained in the traditional medical mode, now offers his patients a multidisciplined approach to healing.

The son of Midwestern farmers, Anderson has come a long way, both geographically and philosophically, from the halls of Indiana University Medical School. Drawn to California in the 1960s, Anderson at first worked in emergency rooms and veterans hospitals, but he found this work discouraging.

John Christopher, Robert Menzies, and Anderson's wife, Sharon Anderson (who did nutritional research), influenced his thinking. But mainly it was his patients who started him on the herbal pathway. After some serious soul-searching, Anderson found a new niche for himself in the world of medicine. He soon added herbs, acupuncture, megavitamins, and nutritional counseling to his professional program. With a successful practice in Mill Valley since 1972, Anderson is encouraged about his work and the alternatives he can now provide.

Jeffry Anderson

All the while I was in medical school, I don't think I heard the term *herb* even once except, perhaps, in some sort of historical context. Maybe they talked about digitalis as coming from foxglove, or reserpine—which is used essentially for hypertension—as coming from rauwolfia, but they never spoke of herbal treatments as such. Of course, we had no training whatsoever in plant identification. As far as I know, there is no medical school in the country that offers that type of background. To learn about herbs, I had to start from scratch.

The way it all happened—what turned my head around—is that I got completely burned out on institutional medicine. After finishing medical school at Indiana University, I spent three or four years at a Kaiser hospital in the emergency room. Then, for another three or four years I served as an attending physician at Port Miley Veterans Hospital in San Francisco. All of this involved a very typical allopathic approach to medicine, which after a while, I found I just couldn't handle. When you work in an institution, you have to do what that particular institution tells you to do even if you don't believe in it. Finally, I came to a point where I wasn't going to do it any longer. I just quit.

I set up a practice in my home in Larkspur. The first year was pretty rough. Things were really slow, but, fortu-

Jeffry Anderson
Mill Valley, California

nately, my wife was working as an x-ray technician, so we got by. Things started to change for the better when I opened an office in Mill Valley.

That was in 1972. All this time I had been really unhappy with allopathic concepts. I knew there was a real deficiency in the system, but I didn't know quite what to do about it. Dealing with toxic drugs and not dealing with nutritional aspects of health just didn't seem to make any sense. But once I opened the office in Mill Valley, I started getting patients who almost refused to take antibiotics and decongestants for colds and infections. At first, this really surprised me. I asked them what they intended to do about it, and they said they were already using herbs. Well, I just kept listening to them and watching the results. People would come in with a sore throat and a cough, and instead of wanting penicillin they would be interested in an herbal combination of, say, goldenseal and licorice root. I soon found that they were having good results without the negative side effects of antibiotics. It was a very practical way for me to find out about herbs.

About this time, I also happened to meet Rob Menzies, and my wife, Sharon, and I took a couple of his classes. Sharon isn't a nutritionist by training, but she grew up on a ranch in Colorado, so outdoor work and a natural way of living always appealed to her. Menzies' classes really got the ball rolling for the both of us. From that point on, I did a lot of reading, I talked things over a great deal with Rob, and after that, I developed my own experimental way of dealing with herbs.

At first I concentrated my herb treatments mainly on home births. I did between 300 and 400 home births in which I used herbs both for prenatal care and the actual birthings. The only problem was that this work eventually became too stressful, so I moved into a strictly holistic practice—without obstetrics. But, by this time, I had a sound footing.

One thing I avoided, and I still don't do, is dispense herbs. I give patients the recipe or the prescription and then I send them to herb stores. Mainly, I don't have the time, the inclination, or the space to have a big herb store. Also, I think there is an ethical consideration involved in selling medicine or nutritional supplements to patients. It can easily seem like a setup. If you see a patient and then prescribe the same herbs that you're going to sell them, you can reap a double profit. So, with few exceptions, where the herbs can't be obtained in any other way, I try to avoid that. Admittedly, however, it may be different in other parts of the country, where you don't find the outlets we have here.

Most of the people in this area are already fairly conscious of alternative methods of healing, and even more so, the people who come to my practice. Chances are, they were referred to me by one of my patients, so they pretty much know what to expect. Of course, a few are always reluctant, so I try to work them into it slowly. It takes time. In general, because the effects of the herbs take longer, people have to make an adjustment to a more natural pace of healing.

I work with almost any form of herb, but I primarily use infusions, where the herb is steeped, and decoctions, where you boil the herbs. The decoctions, of course, are the stronger of the two. Occasionally, I use extracts— where you use various solvents to extract certain properties. With some people the extracts are extremely helpful, particularly with soporifics and sedatives. They are not only easier to take, but they can be highly effective because they're so concentrated. I've used a lot of extracts for certain cases.

To my way of thinking, whatever form is used, the herbs work considerably better on people who modify their diets. In my experience as a practicing M.D., I've found that although a person with a diet that includes a lot of junk food may, in fact, respond to herbal treatments, you'll find a lot greater response when, with a change of diet, their system is less toxic. Sometimes I find that people who lead fairly toxic lifestyles require an antibiotic in addition to the herbs for a particular infection. In these cases, I generally use antibiotics only as a second line of defense—unless it's a very serious infection that could become life-threatening. I always try to encourage non-drug therapy initially. For example, let's say we've got a couple of days. I'll start with a culture—such as a throat or urethral or vaginal culture—wherever the infection seems to localize. Usually, a culture will take 24 to 48 hours to grow, and in the meantime, I'll suggest trying herbs and megavitamin therapy for those two days. By the time the culture is ready, the infection may be either better or gone. If it's not, then the culture will at least tell us what bug it is and which antibiotic will be the most appropriate. Of course some people will say, "I don't want to take the chance. Just give me the antibiotics and I'll take the herbs and vitamins, too." Then I say, "Okay." I'm not "hardcore" in that way, I don't believe in needless rigidity.

With children, however, I try to be a bit more cautious because their systems are obviously going to be more sensitive to side effects and long-term problems with drugs. I work extra hard in trying to convince parents to avoid giving the kid an antibiotic just because he has an earache. For instance, let's take a case of chicken pox. First of all, I would put the child on a diet of fresh fruits and vegetables along with broth and juices—no meat or dairy products. Herbs that I would use internally would include echinacea, aloe vera juice, maybe comfrey and plantain, and sarsaparilla, because it has a mild steroid effect. If there's a lot of congestion, as there often is with chicken pox, I would add the decongestant herbs, such as goldenseal, sage, and mullein. I'll then have the parents make up an herbal decoction or infusion that's really concentrated and mix it with honey. That way it's less like a drink—they can take it in spoonfuls rather than cups. Even with less volume, you'll still get the same effects.

External treatments would depend on what stage the pox lesions are in. When they're fresh, like a fever blister, I'll have people use herbal compresses. The basic three compress herbs are: myrrh, goldenseal, and calendula. And if the lesions itch or feel irritated, I'll usually throw in some sarsaparilla, burdock, or chickweed. I use things like that just for the soothing effect. Plantain's very good, too. People can apply cool, herbal compresses for 5 or 10 minutes and then put aloe vera gel right over it. Let the aloe dry right on the lesion. One treatment which I usually reserve for fever blisters and herpes, but I occasionally use with chicken pox, includes cayenne mixed with the aloe to make a paste. It can be tough on the kids because it burns, but it zaps the lesions really fast. And then, as the lesion is drying up, I usually go into skin treatments of vitamin E and apricot oil, which can be gently massaged right into the scabbing lesion to keep the scarring to a minimum. Jojoba oil is also good for massage, but it's expensive, so a lot of people don't buy it.

Although many herbs are fairly general in their action, I'll use various combinations for different ailments. For example, if I have a patient with an upper nasal sinus infection, I'll recommend a combination of goldenseal root, sage, mullein, and sarsaparilla root. Then I'll usually throw in echinacea because it's a good antiseptic. For a lower respiratory ailment, on the other hand, such as chest congestion or a cough, I use quite a different combination. In that case, I go for licorice root, marshmallow root, sarsaparilla, fenugreek, and cayenne. Once again, I'll add echinacea as an antiseptic.

In addition to basic herbs, I use what might be considered nonherbal adjuncts, such as propolis, which is a resin with which bees line their hives. Propolis is a very effective antiseptic, and an antiviral remedy, which is especially effective for people who get lots of viruses. Although you normally wouldn't consider propolis an herbal remedy, I consider it an adjunct in the sense that it's a natural product which I often combine with herbs.

So far, when it comes to pain, I unfortunately haven't found any really good herbal analgesics that match morphine, Demerol, and Percodan. Although narcotics can be extremely valuable, and we would absolutely be in bad shape without them, I've found a number of people who have unwittingly become addicted to both narcotics and tranquilizers. Tranquilizers are certainly a big problem. Valium is the number one culprit for sure. It's the drug we see the most frequently and yet it has very serious side effects in terms of brain chemistry and neurotransmitter problems. On the other hand, Valium can rid a person of anxiety just fine, but it also can cause severe depression. People using it are often chronically depressed and really are functionally incapacitated. In addition, it's very hard on the liver.

Because Valium is so highly addictive and dependency producing, I try to wean people off of it by using acupuncture and various nutritional supplements such as vitamin B combinations, calcium, and magnesium. Also, I have my own herbal soporific that I have used for years; it's a combination of valerian root, blue vervain, chamomile, catnip, skullcap, and cannibis sativa. Some of those, of course, are fairly potent herbs, so after I've moved people from Valium to herbs, I next try to wean them off of that combination too.

Unfortunately, as far as I know, there is no pharmaceutical company anywhere that's doing serious herbal research except for a few isolated studies of herbal effects on diseases such as cancer. I'm grateful for obvious scientific accomplishments in the research being done in allopathic medicine—such as in cell biology and biochemistry, but we have a desperate need to apply these same energies and techniques to herbs. All the evidence so far indicates that there are multiple factors in a plant's makeup which work together to enhance the therapeutic effects of the desired active ingredient. For example, there may be other enzymes and co-factors that allow a particular ingredient to be absorbed and utilized by the body much more effectively in its plant form than if it's chemically isolated. The problem is that it's going to take several millions of dollars worth of grants and a big laboratory with mass spectrometers and auto-analyzers to prove it. And so far, almost all of our investigative funds are reserved strictly for bio-chemistry research.

I would encourage everyone who's interested in studying herbs to study them any way they can, and if they can't get a certificate or a degree that will qualify them for a license to prescribe herbs, at least they can use them as a nutritional adjunct without officially diagnosing and prescribing. That's how Dr. John Christopher did it for years. He learned the hard way. I know. I spent some time with him a few years ago and he impressed me greatly.

There can be little doubt that the demand for herbal remedies is going to expand, as the consciousness about natural healing expands. Eventually there's going to be a considerable need for herbalists to work with other health practitioners, so I think people who are interested and have the time and financial ability to pursue it should get to work and study as hard as they can. Within 25 or 50 years from now, I imagine that allopathic schools will no longer be running things exclusively. By the year 2000, it may be just the opposite—allopathic medicine will start to wane and some of the alternative approaches will develop more strength. And certainly, qualified herbalists will be greatly in demand.

Guideposts

Herbal Education Centers

American Branch of National Institute of Medical Herbalist
115A Oak Dr.
San Rafael, CA 94901
Specialty: offers one-year course of herbal studies

American Herb Association
P.O. Box 353
Rescue, CA 95672
Specialty: quarterly newsletter, membership discounts

Buckley Wildlife Sanctuary
Rt. 1
Frankfort, KY 40601
Specialty: environmental education and herbal museum
(Ellwood Carr)

California School of Herbal Studies
Box 350
Guerneville, CA 95446
Specialty: herbal education
(Rosemary Gladstar)

Dominion Herbal College
7527 Kingsway
Burnaby, British Columbia V3N 3C1, Canada
Specialty: holistic approach to herbal education, ways of
    growing, gathering, preparing, using herbs

East-West Master Course in Herbology
Box 712
Santa Cruz, CA 95061
Specialty: home study integrating various cultural
    disciplines in herbology

Emerson College of Herbology
11 St. Catherine St. East
Montreal H2X IK3 Canada
Specialty: herbal education

Flower Essence Society
P.O. Box 459
Nevada City, CA 95959
Specialty: seminars, newsletter, Bach remedies

Golden Temple
2322 N. Charles St.
Baltimore, MD 20740
Specialty: herbal healing, Ayurvedic medicine

Green Pines Healing Center
3895 18th St.
San Francisco, CA 94114
Specialty: the tao of herbology, workshops

Green Shores School of British Columbia
Box 46506 Van. Post. Sta. "G"
Vancouver, BC V6R 4G7 Canada
Specialty: residential, correspondence, and apprenticeships
(Norma Myers)

Herb Pharm
347 E. Fork Rd.
Williams, OR 97544
Specialty: apprenticeship training in botanical pharmacy and
therapeutics
(Ed Smith)

Herb Research Foundation
1780 55th St.
Boulder, CO 80301
Specialty: research and education, *Herb News Magazine*

Hygieia College Home Study
P.O. Box 398
Monroe, UT 84754
Specialty: Maiutic (in the manner of a midwife), education of
herbalism and womancraft
(Jeannine Parvati Baker)

The Institute of Traditional Medicine
Rt. 7, Box 50-B3
Santa Fe, NM 87501
(Dr. Vasant Lad)
Specialty: full-time programs in Ayurveda, acupuncture,
herbology, nutrition, and massage

Missouri College of Health Sciences
Rt. 1, Box 14
Centerville, MO 63633
Specialty: herbology courses

National College of Naturopathic Medicine
11231 S.E. Market St.
Portland, OR 97216
Specialty: botanical medicine

National Herbalist Association
219 Carl St.
San Francisco, CA 94117
Specialty: herbal education
(Jeanne Rose)

Oak Valley Herb Farm
Camptonville, CA 95922
Specialty: herb walks, herb retreats, botanical garden
(Kathi Keville)

Pine Mountain Settlement School
Pine Mountain, KY 40810
Specialty: environmental education and annual weekend
    workshops on edible wild and medicinal plants

Platonic Academy
Box 409
Santa Cruz, CA 95061
Specialty: correspondence and tutorial courses
(Dr. Paul Lee)

Rainbow's End Midwifery Study Program
13140 Frati Lane
Sebastopol, CA 95472
Specialty: self education
(Nan Koehler)

Saso's Herb Gardens
14625 Fruitvale Ave.
Saratoga, CA 95070
Specialty: botanical garden, seminars, herbal wreaths
(Louis Saso)

School of Clinical Herbology
905 Alarid St.
Santa Fe, NM 87501
Specialty: clinical herbology

The School of Natural Healing
Box 412 Springville, UT 84663
Specialty: herbology, nutrition, iridology, midwifery,
    reflexology

The School of Natural Healing, London (att. John Morley)
188 Old St.
London EC1, England
Specialty: herbology, nutrition, iridology, reflexology

Smile Herb Shop
4908 Berwyn Rd.
College Park, MD 20740
Specialty: herbal medicine, herb teas, herbs in cooking

Wisconsin School of Natural Healing
312 N. Bassett
Madison, WI 53703
Specialty: herbology, nutrition, iridology, reflexology

YES Educational Society
P.O. Box 4346
Falls Church, VA 22044
Specialty: holistic medicine, personal and social
    transformation

USES

COMMON	BOTANICAL
Angelica	Angelica Archangelica
Anise	Pimpinella Anisum
Basil, Sweet	Ocimum Basilicum
Bay, Sweet	Laurus nobilis
Bergamot (Bee balm)	Monarda didyma
Blackberry	Rubus spp.
Boneset	Eupatorium perfoliatum
Borage	Borago officinalis
Burdock, Great	Arctium lappa
Burnet, Salad	Sanguisorba minor
Camomile, German	Matricaria Chamomilla
Caraway	Carum Carvi
Catnip	Nepeta Cataria spp.
Chervil	Anthriscus Cerefolium
Chicory	Cichorium intybus
Chives	Allium Schoenoprasum
Comfrey	Symphytum officinale
Coriander	Coriandrum sativum
Costmary	Chrysanthemum Balsamita
Dandelion, Common	Taraxacum officinale
Dill	Anethum graveolens
Fennel, Sweet	Foeniculum officinale
Garlic	Allium sativum
Geranium, Scented	Pelargonium spp.
Germander	Teucrium Chamaedrys
Golden Seal	Hydrastis canadensis
Horehound	Marrubium vulgare
Hyssop (Blue Flower)	Hyssopus officinalis
Lamb's Quarters	Chenopodium album
Lavender	Lavandula spp.
Leek	Allium porrum

Herb	Botanical name	Vulnerary	Tonic	Stomachic	Stimulant	Sedative	Laxative	Febrifuge	Expectorant	Diuretic	Diaphoretic	Detergent	Carminative	Astringent	Aromatic	Antispasmodic	Antiseptic	Antiscorbutic
Lemon Balm	*Melissa officinalis*																	
Lovage	*Levisticum officinale*				Whole Plant								Whole Plant		Whole Plant			
Mallow (Marshmallow)	*Althaea officinalis*	Whole Plant																
Marjoram	*Majorana hortensis*																	
Mint family	*Mentha spp.*				Leaves						Leaves		Leaves			Leaves		
Mustard	*Brassica spp.*			Seeds	Seeds													
Nasturtium	*Tropaeolum majus*																	
Oregano	*Origanum vulgare*																	
Parsley	*Petroselinum hortense*		Whole Plant				Whole Plant			Whole Plant			Whole Plant					
Purslane	*Portulace oleracea*																	
Rosemary	*Rosmarinus officinalis*		Leaves	Leaves	Leaves						Leaves		Leaves	Leaves				
Safflower	*Carthamus tinctorius*						Flower				Flower							
Sage	*Salvia officinalis*		Leaves		Leaves			Leaves					Leaves	Leaves				
Savory	*Satureja spp.*												Leaves		Leaves			
Shepherd's Purse	*Capsella bursa-pastoris*	Whole Plant			Whole Plant					Whole Plant								Whole Plant
Tarragon	*Artemisia Dracunculus*														Leaves			
Thyme	*Thymus spp.*		Leaves			Leaves							Leaves			Leaves	Leaves	
Valerian	*Valeriana officinalis*		Root (Whole)			Root (Whole)										Root (Whole)		
Watercress	*Nasturtium officinale*																	Leaves
Woodruff, Sweet	*Asperula oderata*	Leaves		Leaves														
Yarrow	*Achillea millefolium*	Whole Plant	Whole Plant		Whole Plant						Whole Plant			Whole Plant	Whole Plant			

Herb	Botanical name	Vinegars	Teas	Soups/Stews	Sauces	Salads	Confectionery	Butters	Baking	Fragrances	Oils/Shampoos	Drying
Lemon Balm	*Melissa officinalis*		Leaves				Leaves			Leaves		Leaves
Lovage	*Levisticum officinale*						Stem (Whole)					
Mallow (Marshmallow)	*Althaea officinalis*											Root (Whole)
Marjoram	*Majorana hortensis*			Leaves	Leaves	Leaves				Leaves		Leaves
Mint family	*Mentha spp.*		Leaves		Leaves	Leaves	Leaves		Leaves	Leaves	Leaves	Leaves
Mustard	*Brassica spp.*			Leaves	Seeds	Leaves						Seeds
Nasturtium	*Tropaeolum majus*		Flower		Seeds	Leaves	Flower					Seeds
Oregano	*Origanum vulgare*			Leaves	Leaves	Leaves						Leaves
Parsley	*Petroselinum hortense*			Leaves	Leaves	Leaves						
Purslane	*Portulace oleracea*					Whole Plant						
Rosemary	*Rosmarinus officinalis*		Leaves	Leaves	Leaves						Whole Plant	
Safflower	*Carthamus tinctorius*		Flower								Seeds	
Sage	*Salvia officinalis*			Leaves	Leaves	Leaves						Leaves
Savory	*Satureja spp.*	Leaves		Leaves	Leaves	Leaves						Leaves
Shepherd's Purse	*Capsella bursa-pastoris*											Whole Plant
Tarragon	*Artemisia Dracunculus*	Leaves		Leaves	Leaves	Leaves						Leaves
Thyme	*Thymus spp.*			Leaves	Leaves						Leaves	Leaves
Valerian	*Valeriana officinalis*		Root (Whole)									
Watercress	*Nasturtium officinale*					Leaves						
Woodruff, Sweet	*Asperula oderata*									Leaves		
Yarrow	*Achillea millefolium*											

PARTS OF PLANT TO BE HARVESTED

- Berries
- Bulb
- Flower
- Leaves
- Root (Whole)
- Seeds
- Stem (Whole)
- Whole Plant

HOME & GARDEN HERB CHART

Reprinted by permission of *Daily Planet Almanac* (Avon Books).

Favorite Herbal Recipes

*Selections from the Herbal Pathfinders. Presented as
illustrations only. Do not treat any health problem without
the personal guidance of a qualified practitioner.*

Ellwood Carr

MILKWEED BLOSSOM DRINK

25–30 flower heads of common milkweed
$\frac{1}{2}$ cup lemon juice
2 cups water
$\frac{1}{2}$ cup sugar

Gather the fresh, fully opened flowers of the common milkweed *(Asclepias syriaca),* clustered after the dew has dried. In washing the clusters, swish each in water to dislodge insects and any dust, but do not leave in water long enough to dilute the nectar and fragrance of the flower.

Put water and lemon juice in blender and turn to liquefy.

Drop 1 or 2 flower heads in at a time until all are thoroughly pureed.

Heat puree for 5 minutes on low boil. Strain and press out all juice through paper toweling in a sieve.

To the extract, add sugar and enough water to make ½ gallon. Serve chilled.

SASSAFRAS TWIGGY

$\frac{1}{2}$ lb. chopped sassafras twigs
3 qts. water
12–16 vegetable bouillon cubes (in small amount of water
to dissolve)

266

Gather twig end of branches of sassafras trees or shrubs in the dormant season. If leaves are out, strip off the leaves. Cut twigs into 1-inch or smaller pieces. It is best not to use twigs larger than pencil diameter. The larger the twigs, the shorter they should be cut.

Chop the cut twigs a handful at a time in a blender. Cover to avoid flying pieces.

Bring twigs and water to boil and simmer for 5 minutes, stirring to break up the mucilage. Strain through wire strainer or coarse cloth. Return twigs to kettle and add additional quart of hot water and stir to wash out additional mucilage. Strain as before and add to original strained material.

Put all or portions of strained material in muslin straining cloth or towel and tie top tightly. Press liquid through the cloth.

If a very clear product is desired, strain again under pressure and let liquid stand overnight and decant the clear portion.

If product is too ropey, put in blender by portions and liquefy. Add additional water to make 1 gallon.

To each gallon of liquid add 12–16 bouillon cubes (dissolved in water). Serve hot or cold as a drinkable soup.

Recipes from Ellwood Carr, *Weed Patch Cookery* (Chenoa, KY).

John Christopher

COMFREY COMBINATION FOMENTATION

This is an aid for malfunction in bone, flesh, cartilage, and is excellent for varicose veins, sprains, curvature of the spine, tremors, skin eruptions, pulled muscles, blood clots, calcium spurs, etc.

Combine the following herbs: oak bark, marshmallow

root, mullein herb, wormwood, lobelia, scullcap, comfrey root, walnut bark (or leaves), gravel root. Soak the combined herbs in distilled water (at the rate of 1 oz. combined herbs to 1 pint distilled water), for 4 to 6 hours; simmer 30 minutes; strain and then simmer the liquid down to ½ its volume and add ¼ c. vegetable glycerine (if desired). Example: 1 gallon of solution simmered (not boiled) down to 2 quarts and add 1 pint glycerine.

Soak flannel, cotton, or any white material other than synthetics—never use synthetics. Wrap the fomentation (soaked cloth) around the malfunctioning area and cover with plastic to keep it from drying out. Leave on all night six nights a week, until relief appears.

James A. Duke

HERB TEA

1 part catnip
2 parts bee balm
3 parts lemon balm

Mix ingredients well. Pour boiling water over mixture and steep to taste.

HERBAL BOUILLON

1 part chives (leaves)
3 parts pink clover flowers
3 parts chicory flowers

Mix ingredients well. Pour boiling water over mixture and steep to taste.

Root Booster*

4 parts ginger
1 part ginseng
1 part sassafras (may contain safrole)
4 parts sarsaparilla

Mix ingredients well. Pour boiling water over mixture and steep to taste.

*From Jim Duke, *Herbal Vineyard* (Fulton, MD).

Steven Foster

Samuel Thomson's Composition Powder

". . . for the first stages and in less violent attacks of disease."

2 lbs. bayberry-root bark
1 lb. ginger
2 oz. cayenne
2 oz. cloves

Grind all into fine powder, sift through a fine sieve, and mix together well.

Dose: 1 tsp. with 1 tsp. honey dissolved in a cup of boiling water.

From Samuel Thomson, *New Guide to Health or Botanic Family Physician* (Boston: J. Q. Adams, Printer, 1835).

Horseradish Condiment

1 cup fresh horseradish root
$\frac{1}{4}$ cup vinegar
$\frac{1}{4}$ cup olive oil
2 tsp. honey
2 cloves fresh garlic
1 pinch curry powder

Chop root and garlic into small pieces. Place all ingredients in blender. Puree for 2 minutes. Stand back when you open the blender—the fumes are explosive!

Rosemary Gladstar

ST. JOHN'S SALVE

1 oz. St. John's wort flowers and leaves
½ oz. comfrey leaves
2 oz. calendula flowers
1 cup olive oil
¼ cup grated beeswax

Simmer herbs in oil on the lowest heat possible for 20–30 minutes. Keep pan tightly covered. Strain. Add beeswax to herbal oil. Heat just long enough to melt beeswax. At this point 10,000 units of vitamin E and 100,000 units of vitamin A may be added, but are not necessary.

Pour into glass jars and set in a cool place to solidify. This salve will last several months if stored in a cool, shady area. An excellent salve for minor burns, cuts, wounds, and diaper rash.

DREAM PILLOW

1 oz. hops
1 oz. chamomile
1 oz. mugwort
1 oz. lavender
1 oz. roses

Sew dried herbs into small cotton or muslim "pillows"— these are more like a dream sachet. Place next to you as you sleep and watch the panorama of your dreams flow by.

DREAM TEA

You may also like to drink the following tea before bed to inspire dreams:

$\frac{1}{2}$ oz. lavender
1 oz. chamomile
$\frac{1}{2}$ oz. rosemary
$\frac{1}{2}$ oz. damiana
1 oz. peppermint

Mix together. Use 1 tsp. per cup of boiling water and steep 3–5 minutes. Strain.

Carolyn Hutchinson

FEELING FINE TEA BLEND

The herbs in this mixture are chosen so that a balance of minerals and vitamins will be available.

2 oz. each: lemon balm, nettle, parsley, horsetail, alfalfa, chickweed, raspberry, rose hips, peppermint, chamomile, fennel, catnip, comfrey leaf, red clover, oatstraw, spearmint, strawberry leaf, yarrow, shepherd's purse, wintergreen, mullein
1 oz. each: kelp, Irish moss, thyme

Mix all ingredients and store in glass jar. Pour 1 cup boiling water over 1 large tsp. tea. Steep in nonmetal teapot 5 minutes and strain before serving.

Do not use fluoridated water or aluminum cookware for this or any food or beverage if you wish to keep the mineral value intact.

SUPER-SET

—a hair gel for those who still occasionally roll up their tresses.

2 tbsp. Irish moss
2 tsp. rosemary
1½ cups spring, well, or distilled water
1 tsp. cologne (optional)

Boil the herbs and water in an enamel or ceramic pan for 5 minutes or more. Strain into a glass jar to cool; mixture will thicken. Add cologne for scent and as a preservative. Gel will keep a few months. Without cologne (it contains alcohol), the gel will keep about 10 days in the refrigerator.

Keetoowah

COMFREY SALVE

1 part beeswax
2 parts oil
  goldenseal
  comfrey leaves

I don't have a double boiler, so I put the beeswax and oil in a tin can in the middle of a bottle of hot water and then blend them together as they heat up. As the mixture begins to cool, I put in a little goldenseal and comfrey.

I think these things work for everybody: goldenseal, comfrey, oil and beeswax. It is a salve that is helpful for many, many conditions—from poison oak to piles.

Kathi Keville

CALMING BLOSSOM MASSAGE OIL

Take a very clean pint jar and loosely fill it with ½ oz. each of lavender, chamomile, elder, and rose.

Sprinkle 1 tsp. of powdered orris root (a fixative) over them. Pour enough almond oil over the herbs to fill the jar to within an inch of the top (2–3 cups). Pour the oil slowly to allow air bubbles to escape.

Put the lid on the jar firmly and put it in a sunny place. Leave it there and give it a shake once a day. This will keep the oil distributed among the herbs.

In the heat of the summer (85°F), I leave the jar in the sun 5 days. Add 5 days for every 10°F colder. Sunny windows may be quite warm in the winter.

Bring your jar in at a time when it is sun-warmed and will be easy to strain. Hold a wire mesh strainer over a small bowl and pour the oil into it a little at a time, pressing it out of the herbs with the back of a spoon.

Some herb particles will have passed through the strainer, so strain the oil again with a very fine strainer, or coffee or milk filter. A very heavy paper towel will work also. The filter can be folded to fit into a funnel and the oil poured through it.

Heat 3 tbsp. of olive oil in a double boiler and add 1 tsp. of hydrus lanolin, stirring as it melts. Turn off the heat. Add the strained oil and keep stirring. Add 1 tsp. vitamin E oil and ¼ tsp. benzoin tincture (optional).

Bottle, cork, and label your oil. The only thing left to do is find someone to massage!

BATH OILS

Scenting 1 oz. of vegetable oil base with 1 tsp. of essential oil turns it into a bath oil that coats the skin with a silky fragrance. Use 1 tsp. per tub.

For bath salts, add 1 tsp. of essential oil to ½ cup mixed table salt, epsom salts, and borax. Store 1 week in an airtight container to allow the scent to permeate, then package in bottles or individual portions of 2 tbsp. for each bath.

HERBAL HAIR RINSE

> 2 qts. water
> ½ oz. each: burdock, comfrey root, wild cherry bark, and myrrh gum powder
> 1 oz. each: lavender, rosemary, calendula, chamomile, lemon grass, and nettle
> ¼ cup agar-agar dissolved in 1 cup water
> ½ cup cider vinegar

Cook first group of heavier herbs (except for wild cherry bark) for 1 hour on very low heat. Add second group and cook for 15 minutes more. Turn off heat, add wild cherry bark, and let sit until cool. Then strain out the herbs, boil agar-agar water and combine. Add vinegar, and bottle. Once this rinse is opened, it should be refrigerated.

Nan Koehler

BIRTHING TEA

> Equal parts: lavender
> basil
> nutmeg
> red raspberry leaf

Pour boiling water over herb mixture and steep to taste. Don't make it too strong!

Classic Nursing Tea

½ oz. each: marshmallow root
star anise and/or anise seeds and fennel seeds

Place in an enamel pot and simmer with one pint of water for 15 minutes. Add alfalfa, blessed thistle and borage, and steep for 15 minutes. Sip throughout the day.

Vasant Lad

Clove Oil

Boil five whole cloves in one tablespoon of sesame oil. The cloves should remain in the oil. For application, the oil should be warm.

Yogi Tea

2 tsps. fresh grated ginger
4 whole cardamom seeds
8 whole cloves
1 whole cinnamon stick
8 oz. water
1 oz. raw cow's milk, certified

Mix herbs and water. Boil until one-half of the water remains. After the mixture has cooled, add milk and drink. Yogi Tea is used for cold, cough, congestion; as an aid to digestion; and to neutralize toxins in the large intestine.

Paul Lee

Thyme Balm

　200　gm. thyme herb
　　30　ml. oil of thyme (with thymol)
1,000　ml. olive oil
　　　　beeswax

Grind thyme herb *(Thymus vulgaris)* to coarse powder and stir into olive oil. Heat at 100°F for 10 days. Stir every 4 hours. Then strain out herbal oil under pressure and filter through fine cotton muslin.

Preheat herbal oil to 140°F. Add melted beeswax at the ratio of 28 gm. beeswax to 120 ml. herbal oil. Pour in oil of thyme and stir all together until hardened.

Robert Menzies

Brown Rice and Herbal Greens

2　cups brown rice, uncooked
2　tbsp. olive or peanut oil
2　cups water
2　tbsp. sesame seeds
　　pine nuts (optional)
1　lb. dandelion or other fresh greens

Toast brown rice in oil. Add water and place in steamer. (In an automatic steamer, cook about 20–25 minutes.)

When half-cooked, add sesame seeds and a handful of pine nuts (if you can afford or gather them).

Just before serving, add dandelion leaves or other greens, freshly picked and washed carefully. These should be crisp. Cook only 2–3 minutes. Bok choy (chinese cabbage) or spinach may be substituted for the greens.

Rose Petal Salad
(A Small Feast for Four)

  2 cups rose petals, wild preferred
  2 cups mixed dandelion and plantain leaves (very
       tender and young)
  2 cups potatoes, cooked, cooled and diced
  ¼ cup lemon juice or rose petal vinegar
  ½ cup salad oil (fresh pressed olive is nice)
  1 tsp. fresh tarragon
  ½ tsp. sea salt or kelp powder
  ¼ tsp. cayenne pepper
  1 clove garlic, crushed
  2–3 hard boiled eggs (optional)

Gently rub wooden salad bowl with crushed garlic, saving a bit to dash on top later.

Arrange a pretty circle of rose petals, saving some to sprinkle on top. Shred the dandelion and plantain greens on top and add potatoes and eggs.

Stand aside and inhale the essence.

In another bowl, mix together the salad oil, tarragon, lemon juice, sea salt or kelp, cayenne, and the rest of the garlic. Pour this over the salad. Mix with thy heart.

Place the remaining rose petals on top and serve.

Jeannine Parvati Baker

THINGS I USE FOR RELIEF OF BURNS

Ice cold water (to stop burning)
Aloe (to cool and seal—take fresh leaves and apply as a poultice)
Honey (to serve as an antiseptic)
Herb teas taken internally (use in any pleasing combination: comfrey, oatstraw, licorice, cayenne, echinacea, rose hips, parsley)
Herb tinctures (for pain relief—oil of celery seeds, for example)
Herbal baths (use decoction of comfrey root, sow thistle, and comfrey leaves on sterile bandages)
Herbal and saline solution (to soothe exposed tissue)
Apple cider vinegar applied externally (if there are signs of infection; myrrh is also helpful)
Soothing salves (comfrey, calendula)

The wounds must be kept moist, yet not septic. Constant, competent care is required at first.

I also use homeopathy, air ionization, crystal, song, vitamins, lots of non-meat protein such as tofu, polarity balancing, reflexology, color healing, meditation, and psychological healing as well as herbs.

Jeanne Rose

YEGG FORMULA

Some of our best blood-cleansing formulas are composed of herbs that are indigenous to this country. YEGG is my best such formula—I use it for *everything*, or as a tonic to precede any other treatment. It is composed entirely of herbs that the American Indians taught us to use.

    2 parts powdered yellow dock root
    1–2 parts powdered echinacea root
    1 part powdered goldenseal root
    1 part powdered American ginseng root

Mix all ingredients together and encapsulate in size 00 gelatin capsules. When needed, take 2 or 3 capsules 3 times per day for 10 days.

This mixture has been successfully used to help clear up vaginal infections, throat infections, abscessed teeth, and as an aid in overcoming most bacterial and viral infections.

Super Energy Elixir

Helpful in obesity, serious illness of any sort, terminal illness, or cancer. Must be used daily for good health and vigorous vitality and well-being.

$\frac{1}{2}$ cup or more freshly squeezed orange or apple juice (mix the apple juice half and half with mineral water)

2 heaping tbsp. brewer's yeast (it is essential that it be grown on blackstrap molasses for potassium content)

1 heaping tbsp. beet crystals or beet juice concentrate

1 heaping tsp. granular lecithin (make sure it is sweet and fresh)

1 level tsp. vitamin C crystals (ascorbic acid or sodium ascorbate)

$\frac{1}{4}$ tsp. chlorella powder or 3 chlorella tablets

Mix these ingredients thoroughly together in the order given and blend for a moment, if desired. Drink at least 1 glass per day—in serious illness, 3 times per day at regular intervals consistently for at least 6 months. For obesity, mix and drink in place of breakfast and dinner, and for lunch eat a huge salad made from at least 8 vegetables with 10 raw fresh almonds thoroughly chewed. At dinner the overweight person can follow his elixir with some fruit or melon.

This drink is not a substitute for other vitamin and mineral supplementation or for good eating habits. It is not a substitute for water or herb tea taken throughout the day.

LEMON HAND CREAM

almond oil
lemon juice, freshly squeezed
beeswax
lemon oil

Squeeze a lemon and strain through cheesecloth. Pour the juice into a measuring cup and add an equal amount of almond oil. In a small butter melting pot, put a thin piece of beeswax. I use approximately 1 tsp. beeswax for every 3 oz. of cream—this amounts to a thin sheet about an inch square. Add to the pot a bit of the almond oil that has collected above the lemon juice in the measuring cup.

Warm over medium heat gently shaking the pot, about 30 seconds or more. Take the pot on and off the heat so that the wax melts but does not burn. Add the rest of the contents of the measuring cup. Heat, shake, and stir with a wooden spoon until the wax has completely melted. Remove from heat.

Stir with the wooden spoon until cool. Add 1 drop of lemon oil for every oz. of cream. Give it another stir and transfer to a cream jar or bottle. Cap it. Now shake it every few minutes until the cream is completely cold.

Rub a little bit on hands or body whenever needed. This cream is excellent to soften and smooth rough hands. The oil is an emollient, the lemon is a protectant and texturizer.

Lemon Hand Cream is easy to make and takes less than 5 minutes, so make only one lemon's worth at a time. Your measurements then will probably be 1½ oz. lemon juice, 1½ oz. almond oil, 1 tsp. beeswax, and 3 drops lemon oil.

Nam Singh

GINSENG AND OLIVE OIL SAUCE

1 American white ginseng root (6 years old or older)
1 qt. olive oil
½ qt. soy sauce

Place all ingredients in a ½-gal. jar. Put lid on tight and set in a cool, dark place for 1–2 months.

"Herbal" Ed Smith

JUNGLE OIL

1 part oil of wormwood
1 part oil of rosemary
1 part oil of rue
1 part oil of basil

Mix and bottle. I used this in the Amazon jungle as a bug repellent and to draw out the poison of insect stings. Jungle Oil is also a very effective antiseptic and useful against fungus infection and "jungle rot."

Billy Joe Tatum

ROSE BEADS

2 cups fragrant rose petals
1 cup rose geranium leaves

Put petals and leaves into a black iron skillet and cover with water. Simmer 30 minutes (being sure not to boil). Allow to soak. Repeat simmering and soaking for 3 days (add a little water if necessary).

On the 4th day, squeeze out excess water and make a pulp of leaves and petals. Now form beads, either round or square. Make a hole through each bead and gently string beads on a stiff piece of wire (I use a piece of a metal clothes hanger). Dry for several days, turning the beads several times a day, until completely dry.

The beads may now be strung on a satin ribbon or cord and worn as a necklace. Heat from the body allows the black rose beads to give off a rose fragrance. The beads are wonderful for scenting linens, or packed in a suitcase when traveling.

HERBAL BATH

> 1 cup dried comfrey leaves
> 1 cup dried mullein leaves
> 1 cup plantain leaves
> 1 cup peppermint
> $\frac{1}{2}$ cup yarrow leaves and flowers
> $\frac{1}{4}$ cup dried chamomile leaves

Crush and crumble leaves and mix well. Place about ½ cup mixture in a cloth bag and steep 10 minutes in hot water. Add water to bath. Or simply place bag of herbs in hot bath water. This assures one of a fragrant bath which is also soothing and relaxing to tired muscles.

COUGH SYRUP

> 1 tsp. powdered ginger root
> 1 pint hot water
> 1 tbsp. fresh lemon juice
> $\frac{1}{2}$ cup honey

Steep ginger root in water for 10 minutes. Add lemon juice and honey. Sip 4 or 5 times daily when coughing.

Bibliography

Publications by the Herbal Pathfinders

CARR, ELLWOOD. Articles in *Lexington Herald Leader* (Lexington, KY).

———. "Herbal Medicine: Past, Present and Future." Ph.D. dissertation.

———. *Mountain Laurel: A Collection of Recipes.* Pineville, KY: Bell County Homemakers, 1977.

———. "Weed Patch Cookery." Chenoa, KY: Self-published.

CHRISTOPHER, JOHN R. *Capsicum.* Provo, UT: Christopher Publications, 1980.

———. *Childhood Diseases.* Provo, UT: Christopher Publications, 1976.

———. *Dr. Christopher's Natural Healing Newsletter, Vol. I, 1–Vol. III, 3.* Provo, UT: Christopher Publications, 1978–1982.

———. *Dr. Christopher's Three Day Cleansing Program and Mucusless Diet.* Provo, UT: Christopher Publications, 1969.

———. *Just What Is the Word of Wisdom.* Provo UT: Christopher Publications, 1941.

———. *Regenerative Diet.* Provo, UT: Christopher Publications, 1982.

———. *School of Natural Healing.* Provo, UT: Bi World, 1976.

DUKE, JAMES A. *Handbook of Legumes of World Economic Importance.* New York: Plenum Press, 1981.

———. *Isthmian Ethnobotanical Dictionary.* Fulton, MD, 1972.

———. *Medical Plants of the Bible.* Buffalo, NY: Conch Publications, forthcoming.

———, and E. E. Ayensu. *Medical Plants of China.* Algonac, MI: Reference Publishers, forthcoming.

FOSTER, STEVEN. *An Herbal Heresy: The Gentle Art of Herb Culture.* Illustrations by D. D. Dowden. Layton, UT: Peregrine Smith, forthcoming.

KOEHLER, NAN. "Herbs for Woman: An Interview with Nan Koehler." In *The Woman's Encyclopedia of Health and Natural Healing,* by Emrika Padus. Emmaus, PA: Rodale Press, 1981, pp. 290–310.
————. "Mathematical Analysis of Birthing Factors in a Sonoma County Sample." Proceedings of the California Division of the American Association for the Advancement of Science, June 1982. (Reprint available.)
————. "VBAC: Vaginal Births after Cesarean Section." Manuscript available from the author.

Nan Koehler is also working on a book, *A Collection of Information and Stories by Nan Koehler.*

LAD, VASANT. *Ayurveda, the Science of Self Healing: A Practical Guide.* Santa Fe, NM: Lotus Foundation, forthcoming.

LEE, PAUL. Introduction to *The Meaning of Health,* by Paul Tillich. Santa Cruz, CA: Platonic Academy for Herbal Studies; Richmond, CA: North Atlantic Press, 1981.

LUST, JOHN. Introduction to *Back to Eden,* by Jethro Kloss. New York: Benedict Lust Publications, 1980.
————. *About Raw Juices.* New York: Benedict Lust Publications, 1981.
————. *Drink Your Troubles Away.* New York: Benedict Lust Publications, 1981.
————. *The Herb Book.* New York: Benedict Lust Publications, 1974.
————. *Lust for Living.* New York: Benedict Lust Publications, 1959.
————. *The Natural Remedy Bible.* New York: Bantam Books, 1983.

MENZIES, ROBERT. *The Herbal Dinner: A Renaissance of Cooking.* Millbrae, CA: Celestial Arts, 1977.
————. *The Star Herbal.* Millbrae, CA: Celestial Arts, 1980.

MYERS, NORMA. *An Autobiography of an Herbalist.* Duncan, B.C.: G. N. D'Aubigny Company, forthcoming.
————. *The D'Aubigny System of Herbalism: A Twentieth Century System of Herbal Healing.* Duncan, B.C.: G. N. D'Aubigny Company, forthcoming.
————. *Growing the Herbs and Training the Herbalists: The D'Aubigny System of Self-Help.* Duncan, B.C.: G. N. D'Aubigny Company, forthcoming.
————. *Help for Men and Women through Modern Herbalism.* Duncan, B.C.: G. N. D'Aubigny Company, forthcoming.
————. *1000 Case Histories of Herbal Healing.* Duncan, B.C.: G. N. D'Aubigny Company, forthcoming.

PARVATI [BAKER], JEANNINE. *Hygieia: A Woman's Herbal.* Monroe, UT: Freestone Publishing, 1978.
————. *Prenatal Yoga and Natural Birth.* Monroe, UT: Freestone Publishing, 1974.

ROSE, JEANNE. *The Herbal: A Guide to Living.* New York: Bantam Books, 1983.
————. *Herbs & Things: Jeanne Rose's Herbal.* New York: Grosset & Dunlap, 1972.
————. *Jeanne Rose's Herbal Body Book.* New York: Grosset & Dunlap, 1976.
————. *Jeanne Rose's Herbal Guide to Inner Health.* New York: Grosset & Dunlap, 1979.
————. *Kitchen Cosmetics.* San Francisco and Los Angeles: Panjandrum, 1977.

SUN BEAR. *At Home in the Wilderness.* Happy Camp, CA: Naturegraph Publishers, 1968.
————. *Buffalo Hearts.* Spokane, WA: Bear Tribe Publishing, 1969.
SUN BEAR AND WABUN. *The Medicine Wheel: Earth Astrology.* Englewood Cliffs, NJ: Prentice-Hall, 1980.

SUN BEAR; WABUN; NIMIMOSHA et al. *The Bear Tribe's Self-Reliance Book.* Spokane WA: Bear Tribe Publishing, 1978.

TATUM, BILLY JOE. *Wild Foods Cookbook and Field Guide.* New York: Workman Publishing, 1976.
————. *A Field Guide to the Medicinal Plants in the United States.* Peterson Field Guide Series. Boston: Houghton Mifflin, forthcoming.